Mark of the Shark

Mark *of the* SHARK

True Tales

of Terror

from the Deep

Edited by
John Long

FALCON®

GUILFORD, CONNECTICUT
HELENA, MONTANA

AN IMPRINT OF THE GLOBE PEQUOT PRESS

Text design by Casey Shain

Library of Congress Cataloging-in-Publication Data

Mark of the shark : true tales of terror from the deep / edited by John Long.
    p.   c.m.
    Includes bibliographical references.
    ISBN 0-7627-1163-9
    1. Shark attacks. I. Long, John, 1953-

QL638.93 .M37 2002
597.3—dc21

                    2002035445

Manufactured in the United States of America
First Edition/First Printing

"THE RIGHT OF A SHARK TO LIVE after his lights is precisely that of other animated creatures . . . . They belong to one of the world's few really old families. Therefore, if there is anything in priority of possession, the sharks have a much better right to kill us than we have a right to kill them for they have been a long established race ages and ages before we appeared . . . adjusted to our environment with such a close approach to perfection that there has been no necessity for them to change either their structure or their habits in all the passing eons. They preceded us here and the chances are they will survive us. We hate them because we fear them."

—*The New York Times,* July 19, 1916

CONTENTS

Introduction

Over the past couple of summers, perhaps a half dozen beachgoers were attacked by sharks, and both local and national media had a regular feeding frenzy with the various accounts. Survivors turned up on popular talk shows, peeling back clothes and showing off wounds. The radio buzzed with story after story, and for a month or so you could stand in line at most any coastal coffee shop and hear folks talking about "that guy" whose surfboard got chewed in half, or the boy down south who lost his arm. When winter finally came and the swimmers got out of the water, the press held onto the stories much as a shark holds onto its prey, only letting off for a quick breath before printing follow-up articles on the paddleboarder who lost her leg or the free diver who lost his life.

Part of the sensational nature of shark attacks stems from their extreme rarity. The chances of a casual ocean swimmer even seeing a shark are so remote that they approach zero. The odds of an attack increase if you have a bloody nose, wear a wet suit splattered with barbecue sauce, and dive the deep water around Australia's Great Barrier Reef, as one victim did. But regardless of the infrequency of shark attacks, each one is always big news, striking our instinctual mainsprings in a way that hurls us back to when man and beast walked the coast together. And this is troublesome terrain for many people, believing our manifest destiny is to "rise above" the beasts and to shove them to the far edge of consciousness. The result is an "us" versus "them" relationship that bodes poorly for humankind and the natural world and everything in it—especially fierce predators like sharks. Parity with our habitat has slowly given way to a ruinous grab for complete dominion, so much so that Chief Seattle's words—that the earth does not belong to us, but rather, we belong to the earth—have become a tawdry, feel-good slogan for bumper stickers and ad campaigns, spoken out the sides of our mouths between sips of espresso and cell phone folderol. Perhaps only the strike of an indifferent predator can break the trance of this self-absorption.

Technology, security, and social comforts are welcomed by all, but they also shield us from the stark existential facts that we are mortal and that there are natural forces on earth that far surpass our own. Yet beginning with Stone Age paintings on cave walls, right up to modern movies like King Kong and Jaws, predator attack stories have remained an enduring part of human heritage. While the ancient artists focused mainly on the terror and irrevocable effects of the attack, contemporary versions have shifted focus to man showing the creature who's boss after all. Man's victory over Jaws is in effect a fatuous symbolic victory over an existential fact—that we all will eventually die, and if the shark doesn't get us, life eventually will. With the Hollywood article we dance around the fire, and when Rambo or the Air Force finally and inevitably vanquishes the beast, we stroll out of the theater smug as we are fearless. Then the shark strikes once again and we're all talking about it.

At some deep level it's a gut check, these shark attacks (minus the Hollywood ending), and some part of us can't stop talking about them. Many of us seem to require this kind of thing—like some grim medicine we need to swallow to remain fully human. And no question about it, shark attacks are usually grim. Unlike Godzilla or King Kong, the shark typically strikes and slips back into the deep, never to be seen again. Most everyone has something to say about that kind of indifference to almighty mankind. That we can still be eaten alive in "our" very oceans is awesome and terrifying. But there is another side as well, as borne out in many of the stories in this collection.

A shark attack is invariably a quick affair; few last more than a minute. The bulk of "shark attack" stories and accounts are in fact survival narratives. And it is because the survivor and those around him often show such courage and spontaneous resourcefulness that these aspects often outstrip the flashier moment of the actual attack. In a real and human sense, the shark attack often becomes somewhat incidental to the drama and salvation that might follow. The shark is the "hook," the force that puts into motion heroic events that are worth reading and that help redeem us from our eventual decay and the chicanery in which we humans can sometimes immerse ourselves. Ultimately, shark attack stories are about people, their lives, and the valiant lengths to which folks will go to preserve them. When considered in the round, near-death experiences are often life's strongest affirmations, and the stories in this volume seem to confirm that notion.

Over the last fifty or so years, shark advocates—including some who survived near-fatal shark attacks—began campaigns to ensure these marvels of the deep would not be completely wiped out. Something marvelous, terrible, and millions of years old would be lost if the shark were to suffer extinction. There are countless irrefutable philosophical and ecological arguments supporting a preservation stance toward sharks, but perhaps the best argument is the simplest: Every time we kill something off, we murder part of ourselves. If our future relatives are to ever see the light of day, we'll have to leave off trashing our very home and strike some equipoise with the earth and all living things—or both the sharks and ourselves are as good as finished. And it won't be the shark's fault if it ever comes to that.

While I've dashed off a few thoughts about shark attacks, readers will discover their own reasons for reading about them. Working through these pages—which contain the very best shark attack stories drawn from every available source—is a riveting and harrowing adventure, but one, I believe, that celebrates our basic and universal values and shows us what's important in the end. And if you should ever need a quick jolt to snap yourself back to the real world, I trust this volume to convincingly deliver on that count.

The Blood-stained Sea

Hugh Edwards

Australian diving legend Hugh Edwards has not only detailed several riveting shark attacks in the following chapter, he's shined the light of his vast experience on the process of all high-risk sports, making "The Blood-stained Sea" an adventure classic.

Why take the risk? Why take any risk?

As the huge female shark began to circle the cage towards me, there was no time for reflection.

"Peter!"

I had perhaps a couple of seconds to make up my mind. Of course I could jettison the camera, which would free my right hand and enable me to reach the release buckles on the SCUBA harness. Or I could hang on and hope that the shark wasn't hungry.

Letting go of the red case, containing the Beaulieu R16 movie camera which had cost every spare dollar I had, and having the painful experience of seeing it disappear into oblivion, could mean the end of filming. Without it we would probably have to abort the exercise and go home with our tails between our legs. Failure was not a pleasing prospect, particularly if there were to be a suggestion of cowardice attached.

On the other hand, if I continued to cling to the camera and the shark came around the cage and bit my arm off we would still be losers. The red case would go to the bottom anyway and it would be the end of my personal trip on this planet.

Did having your arm ripped off hurt much?

"P-E-T-E-R! For Christ's sake!"

Another burst of bubbles and desperate underwater noise.

The shark was now turning the corner of the cage and as Peter turned with it he looked up as though seeing me for the first time. Realizing my predicament at once, he came across and slowly and carefully unhooked my tank top from the wire mesh. Cool under pressure as always.

Released, the warm flush of relief was almost euphoric. I had a glimpse of the shark disappearing into the distance with a capricious flick of its tail. Why had she abandoned her circumnavigation of the cage I could never tell. But I was certainly glad to see the back of her at that moment.

Closer to hand, Peter was giving me the diver's finger-and-thumb sign: "Are you OK?"

I responded, "I am OK."

Yeah, just fine. . . .

But my heartbeat was at a machine-gun rate. My hand shook as I readjusted the camera aperture. A lesson had been learned, and fortunately not the hard way. From that time on we would secure our tanks on the mesh barrier of the cage with octopus straps, and be free to move about without tank or harness. We had to double the length of our regulator hoses, but the move prevented the possibility of getting hooked up again.

We also stopped using fins, since these also are too cumbersome in the cage. Instead we put mini-weightbelts around our ankles, three kilograms on each. Together with our standard eight-kilo waist-weightbelts the foot-weights made for better balance. The ingenuity, the ability to improve our situation, was one of the differences between ourselves and the sharks we had come to study.

Sharks are born perfectly evolved to fill their place in the ocean. They come into the world equipped with all the instinctive knowledge they will ever need to live out their predatory lives. They are the product of sixty million years of evolution.

In contrast, we *Homo sapiens* are physically insignificant creatures. But this weakness has turned out to be a long-term strength. To survive, our ancestors had to use their hands and brains. They learned to improvise, to utilize artificial means to make them strong. Now facing the Great Whites, we epitomized the rise of *Homo sapiens*. We had a boat to carry us; SCUBA to breathe underwater; wet suits to keep us warm; cameras to capture the images of the sharks on film; the television systems that would send the same sharks swimming through to thousands of homes in different parts of the world. . . . These were all part of the miraculous technical advances of modern life.

So much, in fact, has happened in our own lifetime. Television, computers, space travel, the invention of SCUBA equipment that allows us to breathe underwater and study the sharks so closely—all of these were unknown when I was born.

But our bodies inside the wet suits, hearts beating hard at the sight of the predator, were essentially similar to those of the animals around us. The sharks, the whales, the dolphins in the Sound. The albatrosses and black petrels and skua gulls which clamored around the dead whales . . . Each species had evolved in its own unique way to fill niches in the environment of land, sea or air. Naked, we were just another creature on the earth. Prey or predator.

Why take the risk?

Why take ourselves back a few thousand years to the daily situation of ancestors who regularly faced being eaten by stronger predators? Who could not even dream of the safety and security we enjoyed as their more technically literate descendants? It was a question we asked ourselves at times of stress. "What the bloody hell am I doing here?"—as a shark struck the cage and sent it spinning we fell in a sorry heap on the mesh floor.

It was a rhetorical question and, once the stress situation was resolved and we had ceased being animals trying to survive a predator attack, we were again the technically superior species able to rationalize our behavior. A rationale which would have seemed incomprehensible to a shark, and indeed to a large percentage of our own human species.

The great British mountaineer Leigh Mallory, who attempted to climb Mt. Everest on nine occasions, was asked why he did it. Why he continued to risk his life on what was essentially just a bigger and more lethal snowbound rock.

"Because it's there," he said.

Humans do things far outside the scope of ordinary species' behavior. For other animals life is basically a matter of finding food and shelter, breeding, and surviving. That is the difference between *Homo sapiens* and the other animals. We do all kinds of crazy and sometimes unnecessarily life-threatening things beyond the primary requirement. Like mountaineering, and getting too close to sharks. The need to do these things is mental rather that physical. The mind drives the body.

Curiosity, the desire for knowledge and experience out of the ordinary, is one of humankind's characteristic traits. Curiosity, basically, was what had got us into the shark cage. The challenge was what kept us there, and the possibility of some future financial return hardly came into consideration.

"Curiosity," I also reminded myself from time to time "killed the cat." I was never sure where the old saying came from—along with the "tradition" that a cat has nine lives. We were reminded often enough in the shark cage that we humans had only one life to trifle with. High on Mt. Everest, on June 8, 1924, closer to the peak than anyone had ever climbed before, Leigh Mallory finally lost his life. His body was never found.

"What are you trying to prove?" That was another question he may have been able to answer on that sun-sparkling day in the snow with the summit in sight. His companions later speculated that he may have made it to the top, only to fall victim to the mountain on the euphoric descent. What an irony if it were true!

But if someone *needed* to ask that question of why he was there, then there was no answer that would satisfy them. In our case, to paraphrase Leigh Mallory, the sharks were there. But the questioner would still not understand.

It was not about proving we were braver or better than anyone else. Courage is often a matter of circumstance. I get nervous climbing the 150 foot (46 meter) mast of the sail training ship *Leeuwin*. Or sitting in a motor car driven by someone else at 150 kilometers per hour. A bucking horse is not really my idea of fun and just watching bungee jumping on television makes my toes curl. The sea, on the other hand, is a familiar environment for me and has been so since childhood. But with familiarity comes the knowledge that the sea has many moods and strengths that must be respected. Where the ocean is concerned there is a limited future for risk-takers. I always remember the lore of fisherfolk:

> *Those who be not afraid of the sea will soon be drowned. For they will put to sea on a day that they should have stayed ashore.*
> *But those of us who be afraid of the sea be only drowned now and again.*

or the helmet divers' traditional caution:

> *There are old divers and bold divers*
> *But no old bold divers.*

We took pains to eliminate as many of the risks as possible in filming the sharks. The operation could never be 100 percent safe because of the unforeseen. There was also no opportunity for preliminary testing to find the weaknesses. You can't have a practice run with Great White sharks. It is the real thing or nothing.

If there were any possibility of complacency creeping into our daily stints in the shark cage, we needed only to recollect what had happened to others in less favorable circumstances.

It was true that the sharks sometimes looked so beautiful, so majestic cruising past the cage with golden dapples of sunlight on their backs that the sense of danger receded. There was an occasional irrational urge to swim out through the camera gap and dance with them.

But when our sharks came so close that we could touch them, when we saw the rows of ivory daggers in their mouths, and looked deep into their eyes then we read something there that made us shiver in our wet suits.

It was a sense of implacable and merciless purpose. To those watching from the boat above the sharks looked so graceful that their smooth beauty of movement was sometimes confused with benign motivation.

"Aren't they gentle?" someone suggested.

Again, it was a case of the eye deceiving the head. Polar bears look cuddly, too. But they are efficient terrestrial carnivores, eating seals and people too, if they can catch them. The blood and entrails crimson in the snow, belie the beauty of the beast. In the cage we were closer than those above the silver surface, and we looked directly into the dark eye of *Carcharodon carcharias*. What we read there was far from gentle.

It was also suggested by a visitor that since the sharks appeared so "safe" we should abandon the safety of the cage and swim freely with them.

Why not?

"It's up to you guys," said Vic Martin, the surface cameraman, hopefully. "But it would be a World First. Great film!"

We thought about it. Worked out how it could be done. And what could go wrong. Having something go wrong, of course, would make the "best" film of all. A guaranteed sale in every country that sported a television network. Terrific, from a production point of view, we agreed. Just so long as it was someone else who got chopped up in those particularly efficient predatorial jaws.

A Great White shark attack is not a pretty sight. There is so much blood in the human body.

During the preceding decade there have been a series of horrific attacks on Australia's southeastern coast, and as divers we probably related more closely to them than those who stayed dry on the deck of the boat above. We were also that critical distance closer to *Carcharodon* in the physical sense.

The first of the attacks, which shocked all Australian divers, was at Aldinga Beach in South Australia. With its fringing reef, Aldinga lies in St. Vincent's Gulf, about 88 kilometers south of Adelaide. It is one of a series of southern curving beaches with high red bluffs on the peninsula that ends with Cape Jervis; Kangaroo Island standing high across the water.

Aldinga is a pleasant beach, a favorite with families and, up to the 1960s regarding as entirely safe from sharks. The offshore reefs provide good ground for fishing and it used to be a popular choice for spearfishing competitions because it pleased both the reef-swimming divers and their friends and families who spent the day on the beach.

The area's notoriety began on Sunday March 12, 1961, when the Cuda Spearfishing Club and the Underwater Sporting and Photographic Association were holding their annual spearfishing competition.

The president of the Association, a South Australian State champion and one of Australia's top competitive divers, was Brian Rodger. At twenty-one years of age, 2.3 meters in height with a huge frame and impressive physique, he was at a physical peak after a summer-long diet and exercise program.

South Australia's last shark attack had been in 1946 and only three other attacks had been recorded since 1836. It was thought that divers were immune to shark attack—though there had been occasional incidents when whaler sharks stole speared fish from the floats that divers trailed behind them. But they were regarded as being more of a nuisance than a danger.

Only the week before at Aldinga, Brian Rodger had a 2.7 meter whaler—the biggest shark he had seen up to that time—make a pass at his fish as he was threading one on to his float. And another shark of unknown size had gobbled 23 kilos of fish, plus a pair of plastic shoes, off another diver's float.

Rodger remembered being annoyed about that incident because the shoes had belonged to him. But at the time, the size of a shark which could bolt down all that fish (and the shoes) in one mouthful carried no significance for him.

On the Sunday, the competition was drawing to a close. By lunchtime, after four and a half hours in the water, Rodger already had a good bag of fish. About 2:30 P.M. he was making his way back toward the shore a kilometer distant. Suddenly he was surprised to see two large mulloway kingfish, 25 to 30 kilos in weight, flash beneath him.

"Now there's an unusual thing," he thought. In his years of diving in South Australian waters he had not seen these kingfish in open water before. They passed too quickly for a shot. But there was always the chance they would come back, since kingfish are inquisitive creatures. He prepared to dive after them, relaxing to take a good deep breath, when suddenly he screamed through his snorkel. Something sharp and ragged and terribly heavy had struck him with tremendous force, throwing his whole body into a fearful spasm of pain.

He felt the pressure of a tremendous weight and was aware that something huge had seized his leg and hip. It was shaking him violently from side to side.

As the teeth tore through flesh and sinew he twisted round to find himself looking into the black eye of a Great White shark, which had the lower part of his body gripped in its jaws.

"I read once about jabbing a thumb into a shark's eye to make him let go, and tried to reach around with my left arm. Instead of getting his eye I jammed it down his throat, and slashed the arm to the bone on his upper teeth. . . .

"You'll have to be good to get out of this one!" I thought.

"Surprisingly the shark did let go, and then came back in a fast, tight circle for another bite. That was really terrifying because now I could see the whole shark and the size and enormous power of him.

"But at least I had my gun and now I had room to use it. As he came around I slammed a spear into the top of his head, about 7 centimeters behind the eye. . . .

"It hit him hard, stopping his charge while he threw his head from side to side to shake out the 1.5 meter stainless steel spear. He managed this soon enough. But it was strange how even though I knew I was badly hurt myself I got a thrill from planting the spear into something so large and powerful.

"It was quite irrational, but for a moment that was all that mattered and I felt pleased and excited.

"Then his tail flicked away into the murk, and left on my own I realized just how serious my position was. Looking down at my leg laid open to the bone—in enormous rents from which the blood clouded—and at my shredded and lacerated arm, I knew that unless I could stop the bleeding I wouldn't make the distant shore. The actual wounds wouldn't kill me. But the loss of blood would.

"For a moment or two I wasn't sure what to do. But I found, astonishingly enough, that I could still move my leg, and I figured that if I could swim maybe I still had a chance of making shore.

"I'd done a first aid program as part of the State's Underwater Emergency Rescue Squad course, and the knowledge I'd picked up there was pretty useful.

"About halfway back to the beach I realized that I was weakening from loss of blood. It occurred to me that the rubber from my spear gun made a natural tourniquet, and I twisted it tight over my upper thigh with my knife, jamming the handle under the bottom of my wet suit jacket. That stopped the blood flow a bit, and I began the longest swim of my life.

"It seemed to take forever. I kept watching the beach, and it didn't seem to be coming any closer. Gradually I was getting weaker and weaker.

"I'd ditched my gun and lead-belt and the float with all my fish. I hated doing it. Silly how a few points for a competition with a few dollars' worth of gear still seemed so important when my own life was at stake. The fish float was borrowed and I had to really force myself to abandon that.

"So I plodded along, weaker and weaker, keeping going until it became difficult to breathe even through a snorkel. I rolled on my back and kicked along that way for a while.

"As the land came closer it looked beautiful. I wave and yelled, 'Shark!'

"But it seemed to have no effect on the people on the beach. I was about at the end of my strength and was just despairing at the waste of vital energy when a rowboat appeared with two young spearfishermen rowing for all they were worth.

"'Hang on! We'll be right with you!'

"It was only a 7 foot [2.1 meter] boat. I'm pretty big and heavy and it was obvious we couldn't all fit in. Without hesitation one of them jumped out into the bloodied water—where the shark might still have been lurking for all he knew—and helped heave me in. He swam behind pushing to help the boat along. Pretty brave stuff, I thought.

"From then on everything was OK. A whole lot of divers ran across the reef and picked the boat up bodily to carry it to shore. There was a St. John's Ambulance man there. They rigged an old door as a stretcher and hauled me up the cliff—white and blue around the face by this time from loss of blood—and the police organized an ambulance dash to Royal Adelaide Hospital."

Rodger had lost four liters of blood. Only his strength and fitness saw him through. He had more than 200 stitches in a three-hour operation.

The effectiveness of the repair work done by Dr. Matuzek and Dr. Hyde was shown when, after sixteen days in the hospital and two months recuperating at home, Rodger was back diving again. Later in 1961, he set a new Australian free-diving record by swimming down 45.4 meters (149 feet) in a Mt. Gambier lake, on a single breath. A year later he ran a close second to Ron Taylor, later world champion, in the Australian Spearfishing Championships in Western Australia, and won the championship aggregate.

Rodger's attack, not surprisingly, shook the confidence of South Australian divers. But as the months passed the memory faded and it began to be treated as a freak occurrence, unlikely to be repeated.

A perception that was to change dramatically in the following year.

On Sunday, December 10, 1962, sixteen-year-old Jeff Corner and a friend, Allen Phillips, were taking part in a spearfishing competition at Caracalinga Head, 22 kilometers south of Aldinga where Brian Rodger had been attacked in the previous year. Jeff Corner, the South Australian junior champion, and Phillips were swimming about 182 meters offshore with a surf ski, in water about 8 meters deep and with fair visibility, about 1 P.M.

Phillips had just dived not far from Corner, looking for crayfish, when he saw a disturbance in the water near his friend. At first he was pleased, thinking Corner had speared a large fish—then he saw the tail of a big shark break water.

"Probably pinching fish off the boat," he thought, but as he swam across and ran into a welling cloud of blood he realized with dread certainty what had happened.

He turned and swam for their surf ski nearby, then desperately paddled to Corner who was surrounded by a pool of his own blood, with the shark gripping his leg.

"I grabbed Jeff and tried to pull him onto the ski. But the shark, which I recognized at once as a White Pointer from its pointed snout and black eye, tugged him down and out of my grasp, under the ski.

"Jeff came up again on the other side of the ski, and I caught him by the shoulders. The shark still refused to let go, and I banged it with the paddles. Hard."

"Then for no special reason it released its grip and just lay on the surface watching us. I tried to pull Jeff onto the ski. He just looked at me, unable to speak, and his eyes rolled back. I think he was dead then. His leg was terribly mutilated, stripped of flesh from the hip to the knee.

"The White Pointer just lay there and watched, cold and calculating. I cut the fish off the float and threw them over to distract him, but he took no notice of them, just kept watching us. Then I found Jeff's handspear was stuck in his good leg, and jerked it free and prodded the shark with it. But he didn't even seem to feel it.

"I couldn't get Jeff right onto the ski, and so I paddled for all I was worth with one leg hooked round his body. The shark followed. At any moment it could have made a rush and tipped us over, or dragged us off the ski.

"Then another spearfisherman, Murray Brampton, came paddling across on a ski.

"'Keep going!' he shouted, and I saw him lift his paddle and bang it down on the shark. That gave us the break we needed.

"Soon after, I reached the beach, and they said Jeff was dead."

Corner's parents and Phillip's own wife and child were on the beach.

A year later, on another Sunday morning, December 8, 1963, the third attack in the series took place.

This time the scene was Aldinga again, close to the spot where Brian Rodger was attacked in 1961, and the occasion was the 1963 South Australian State Spearfishing Championships. The victim was Rodney Fox, the 1962 South Australian champion, strongly favored to retain his title in 1963.

It may be that he had unwittingly saved Rodger's life in 1961. Fox was swimming near him when Brian was attacked and though he was unaware of Rodger's desperate situation he himself was circled by a large and aggressive Great White which came so close at times that he could have touched it with his gun. He kept diving to the bottom, edging shorewards, and the shark stayed with him ten minutes or more.

Fox thought later that it was probably the shark that had attacked

Rodger, following the now-diffused blood trail. The distraction offered unintentionally by Rodney Fox may have allowed Rodger to escape.

In 1963 at Aldinga, Fox was about a kilometer from shore, on the edge of a deepwater drop-off from 7 to 18 meters, with less than an hour of the competition left to go. As his finger tensed on the trigger he sensed, rather than felt, everything go still in the water around him.

"It was a silence. A perceptible hush . . . Then something huge hit me on the left side with enormous force and surged me through the water. I knew at once from the previous incidents what had happened—and was dazed with horror.

"I felt sick, nauseous. My mask was knocked off, and everything was blurred and there was a queer sensation as though all my insides were squeezed over to one side. I reached out behind and groped for the shark's eyes. At that point it let go of me, and I pushed my arm down its throat by accident.

"With the release of the pressure uncontrollable agony swept over me in waves. But at least I was free. As I kicked for the surface and air I felt the shark under my flippers all the way. As I gulped air I felt the scrape of his hide and wrapped myself around him so he couldn't bite again.

"The shark took me back to the bottom. We rolled around scraping rocks and weed and I let go, desperate again for air.

"On the surface there was red everywhere. My own blood. And through it the head of the shark appeared, conical snout, great rolling body like a rust-colored tree trunk.

"Indescribable terror flowed through my body, but just before it reached me, it veered away and I felt the tug of the fish float on my belt. The shark had grabbed my fish float and suddenly I was jerked below again, and towed 10 to 12 meters or more on my own line. It seemed ridiculous to die of drowning after all I'd been through. But my fumbling fingers couldn't undo the belt to which the line was attached.

"Then the line parted—perhaps on the shark's teeth—and I floated up to the surface. . . ."

At Aldinga that year, 1963, because of the previous attacks the organizers of the competition had boats picking up competitors' catches in order to avoid attracting sharks.

A boat was close to Fox, whose total of fish already made him a likely winner, when they heard the scream, "Shark! . . . Shark!" and saw him threshing in blood-stained water.

They dragged Fox into the boat and the men there, friends of his, were almost sick when they saw the extent of his injuries. His rib cage, lungs, and upper stomach were exposed, with great flaps of skin and sinew flayed back. His arm was ripped to the bone. His lungs were punctured, the ribs crushed from the enormous bite of the shark.

His friend Bruce Farley kept him bending forwards, huddled in the bow of the boat to keep the wounds closed.

"We knew he was bad. But we didn't open up his wet suit to find out the full extent. We made that mistake with Brian Rodger in 1961 and his leg fell apart." Keeping the suit on was to be a vital factor.

Farley organized the beach rescue, finding a policeman almost as soon as he jumped ashore. "He knew all the right numbers to ring." They got Fox into a private car and began driving him toward Adelaide while an ambulance dashed south to meet them. He was in the hospital, 55 kilometers away, less than an hour after being picked up by the boat. He was lucky enough to find a surgeon on duty who had returned that day from doing a specialized course on chest operations in England.

Rasping and choking on his own blood, Fox was so close to death that he heard someone at the hospital suggesting they should call a priest.

"But I'm a Protestant," he choked indignantly, before the significance of the suggestion sank in.

Fox's toughness and physical fitness carried him through. But there is no doubt that if it had not been for the speed with which he and Brian Rodger were got to the operating theater they would have shared Jeff Corner's fate. Both were on their last reserves of strength with such severe loss of blood that another hour without expert aid and transfusion would surely have been too much even for their exceptional constitutions.

It was significant that neither of them went into shock—a factor which kills many shark victims. Apart from their superb physical fitness this may have been because, as divers, they were familiar with sharks and had, without realizing it, psychologically prepared themselves for surviving an attack.

In 1964 the South Australians won the Australian Spearfishing Championship teams event. In the South Australian team were Brian Rodger, Bruce Farley, and Rodney Fox.

With Fox's experience the series of Great White shark attacks in St. Vincent's Gulf ended. It may have been partly because the third attack was the last straw for many South Australian divers, who turned to safer sports. Spearfishing competitors dwindled down in numbers to a few diehards. Or it may simply have been part of the unpredictable pattern of attacks experienced in other parts of the world. No one really knows why they start, or why they stop. Except the sharks.

Shark attacks, like those in South Australia, attract all kinds of theories. The common factors at Aldinga and Caracalinga were spearfishing competitions. Ironically, all of the victims were champions, seized, possibly, because they were swimming furthest out.

It seemed likely on analysis of the attacks that the sharks had been attracted by the blood and vibrations from the struggling fish. This was a comforting thought for divers using SCUBA and who were more interested in photographing fish than killing them.

"No blood, no sharks." That was the general opinion.

But with sharks, and especially the Great White, it seemed that as soon as people believed they knew their behavior patterns the sharks did something different.

Henri Bource, a Melbourne musician aged twenty-five in 1964, was a keen underwater photographer. For Henri, November 26, 1964, began as a pleasant sort of day, the kind he most looked forward to. With forty other divers and friends from several clubs, including his own Victorian Aqualung Club, he was one of a party aboard the fishing boat *Raemur-K*.

They were heading out from Port Fairy bound for Lady Julia Percy Island and the deck was crowded with divers and their gear. It was a scene typical of many weekend dives as they approached the island. People struggling into wet suits, adjusting harnesses, fiddling with gauges and loading cameras. All the last minute things.

Henri, who was meticulous, had his gear ready early. In fact, most of it had been ready long before the trip. In the wheelhouse of the fishing boat he listened to the skipper Walter Kelly talking about the island with its colony of seals. The conversation inevitably turned to sharks. "I've seen some big ones out here from this boat," said Kelly, telling them about some of his experiences. "There's one in particular called Big Ben. He's been hanging around here for years."

Henri Bource had never seen a shark previously, and had no reason to be afraid of them. He was fascinated by the fisherman's account and one of his ambitions was to get a really good shark sequence on film with his camera.

They reached the island, about 8 kilometers offshore and 22 kilometers from Port Fairy, an hour and a half after leaving the wharf. Kelly dropped anchor in the bay of the lee of Lady Julia Percy. The island was rocky with spectacular cliffs, and there were at least a thousand seals on the lower slopes. The acrid smell of ammoniac seal droppings drifted offshore on the light breeze.

The fur seals set up a tremendous din, barking, squealing, and baying, as the boat approached. When Kelly anchored about 180 meters offshore, scores of them splashed into the sea and came out to meet them. "It was everything an underwater photographer could wish for," Henri recalled, "and I could hardly wait to get into the water."

The first divers were soon sporting with the seals.

Henri's time of entry was listed as 12:45 P.M. by his girlfriend Jill Ratcliffe, who was safety officer for the day. The club's safety regulations required him to swim with a partner if he wanted to use breathing apparatus. Since he was keen to a get a camera record of the seals, and preferred to go on his own, he went free-diving with a snorkel.

But the visibility was disappointing so he decided to change his technique, instead silhouetting the seals against the surface to get a better result.

"The visibility was even worse than I had thought. But the seals were helpful. I kept diving to a small ledge just below the rock and there I was able to film a number of seal cows, as they darted and spiraled through the long strands of kelp.

"All too soon I was out of film, so I swam back to the boat."

He had hoped Jill would be able to have a dive. But at 1:30 P.M. she was still logging other divers and he decided to do some more free-diving with the seals, joining two other snorkel divers, Fred Arndt and Dietmar Kruppa. Together they found a large bull seal floating on the surface, lying on his back with a hind flipper sticking out of the water, and soaking in the sun. A seal at peace with the world.

"When we turned up he rolled a wary eye at the three of us but seemed too lazy to move. Fred was the first to actually touch him. After a cautious ten minutes he accepted Dietmar and myself as well. It was one of those rare moments of communication with wild creatures. We thought it was pretty wonderful. Something to tell the others when we got back."

They began diving with him, and scratching him under the flippers. Suddenly without warning the bull and all the nearby seals disappeared.

"The water was quite empty. There was a split second of eerie silence, and our instinct as divers warned us that something was wrong."

They dived down about 10 meters again, hugging the bottom and looking around them. But they could not locate the seals.

"The premonition of imminent trouble was still very strong and as I came to the surface I lifted my head out of the water, looking around to locate Fred and Dietmar. I was going to suggest that we'd better get back to the safety of the boat.

"Without any warning something hit me with tremendous force. I threw my arm up in the diver's signal for 'Help!' and screamed 'Shark . . . Shark!'

"I was torn through the water with enormous power and dragged below. The force of the attack ripped off my mask and snorkel. I could only make out a blurred shape, a huge shadow, as the shark took me down to the bottom, gripping me by the leg.

"As it dived deep, the shark shook me the way a dog would shake an old slipper. The pain was unbearable. I found myself reaching for the shark's eyes in a desperate attempt to escape. But I could barely reach my arm around his gigantic snout, and I just scrabbled helplessly across the monster's muzzle.

"There was another sensation in which the pain and fear were almost forgotten. I was drowning. I needed air—suffocating as I was tugged and rolled from side to side.

"Then suddenly it all stopped. The shaking and the turmoil ceased.

"There was a moment almost of peace. Then I realized, as I groped for the surface, that I had just had my leg bitten off.

"The air was wonderful as I gasped on the surface. Then I felt down to the remains of my left leg. I was quite calm. Shock, perhaps. But I found it hard to focus clearly. There was a curious division in which my body tended toward natural animal panic. But my mind remained quite detached."

Dietmar Kruppa was the first to Henri's side. The injured diver clutched at his shoulder, trying to catch his breath. He tried to speak but no words came. The blood tasted sweet in his mouth as it clouded the water. Then he realized the shark would attack again and, afraid they would not be able to see it coming in the blood, he tried to push himself away from Dietmar so that he would not be hit too.

The shark came back at least five times. But Fred Arndt and Dietmar Kruppa showed tremendous courage, fighting the monster off with their light metal handspears. They were spears meant for little fish, not sharks a ton in weight. The spears were bent and twisted afterwards. But despite their repeated jabs the shark did not attack either Arndt or Kruppa.

Now the *Raemur-K* was bearing down on them.

As soon as the cry "Shark!" was heard and the welling cloud of blood was seen from the boat, Walter Kelly had hit the starter button of the motor and surged the boat toward them without even waiting to pick up the anchor. He dragged it with the boat's power. As they drew close, Jill Ratcliffe grabbed the safety line and without hesitation jumped in and swam toward the struggling group in the blood-stained water. Others jumped in alongside her with no thought of their own safety.

At the side of the boat, Jill called for a rope. Quickly, two of the divers entered the water and fastened the line around Henri. But they couldn't lift his weight out of the water. "In a last desperate attempt," Henri recalled, "I slid my arm up the rope, and I felt a hard grip on my wrist. Colin Watson, a policeman, grabbed my arm and jerked me on board, spraying blood across the deck."

The sight was almost too much for some of the others on board, who had been unaware that Henri Bource had lost his leg. It was hardly pleasant for those in the water. Apart from what must have been a ghastly sight, they realized they were left in the water in a pool of blood with the shark still around.

Colin Watson and the others carried Henri to the middle of the deck and immediately began to apply a tourniquet and first aid.

"I remember only the dark shapes of wet suits and the occasional face above me, registering horror. Not until the moment I'd been taken on board did anyone realize the terrible extent of my injury. The shark had severed my leg at the knee.

"My most vivid recollections now are of the faces; they all looked at me with disbelief. Their shocked expressions seemed to say: 'This couldn't be happening. This is the sort of thing you only read about!'"

Despite the horror of the situation the helpers' first aid was coolly and efficiently applied, and the swift placing of the tourniquet was to prove vital in the drama that followed. There was an agony of indecision while they decided whether to pick up people who were still on the island. They decided to head for port and explain later. Then, on the way back to Port Fairy, Walter Kelly dodged through reefs and lines of cray-pots on the shortest possible route home. As it turned out, every minute counted in what was literally a race for Henri Bource's life. After the cruel ill-chance of the encounter with the shark he did have some lucky breaks.

By the time they got under way the initial shock had diminished and Henri could distinguish voices. Somebody was at the radio, calling for an ambulance and a doctor to be standing by at the Port Fairy land-ing. He heard them tell the shore-based operator that his blood group was unknown. Lifting his head a little, he managed to whisper the blood group to somebody above him and a moment later heard it radioed ashore. This was one of the things which made the hairline of difference between life and death.

Strangely his mind was still clear, and he was aware of the people around him. But his vision was fading, and as his strength ebbed from shock and loss of blood, he knew he was approaching closer to death.

An ambulance met the *Raemur-K* at the wharf. Henri's next sensation was of the rubber suit being cut away from his arm, then a needle being inserted to allow him to receive a life-sustaining transfusion.

Henri did not know at this stage but he had lost 3.5 liters of blood. Taken from the normal 4.5 liters held in the human system, it didn't leave much to go on with. Doctors said later that if the journey had taken a little longer, or if he had lost a fraction more blood, he would have passed the point of no return.

The ambulance rushed him to the new Warrnambool Hospital.

From there on Henri's recollections were hazy. A hospital corridor. The faces of nurses looking down at him. The rubber suit being cut away. "That hurt a bit because it had cost hard earned savings."

When he awoke from the anesthetic of the operating theater, it was still only nineteen hours since the shark had gripped his leg.

As consciousness returned he became aware of a cage holding the bedclothes high at one end of the bed. It covered an empty space, the place where only the day before Henri Bource's leg had been.

"My leg had gone and there wasn't a damned thing I could do about it."

There were a number of common factors in these attacks on divers in southeastern Australia.

All of them were in cold water locations. They were contrary to accepted wisdom which believed that shark attacks were triggered by warm water and rising temperatures. No one knew at the time that some sharks, including the Great White, are warmblooded.

None of the victims saw the shark before they were hit. *Carcharodon* apparently had the ability to charge from outside the divers' vision and to catch them unawares. All who survived remarked on the severity and disorienting effect of the impact.

"You don't see the shark that gets you!" became a grim divers' maxim in southern Australian waters.

Another interesting statistic was that all the survivors—who might have been expected to quit the ocean and go no deeper than a bathtub for the rest of their lives—actually went diving again.

Brian Rodger and Rodney Fox became spearfishing champions on the national scene. Bruce Farley, who helped save Fox's life, became one of the most successful pearl divers in Broome in Western Australia. Henri Bource overcame the loss of his left leg to become an underwater welding specialist on oil rigs in Bass Strait. Lee Warner, who had witnessed Bob Bartle's horrific death, became an abalone diver in the Great Australian Bight—that cold kelp-grown coast, where Great White sharks are most frequently found.

None of them would ever forget the incidents with which they were involved. The shadow was always there, even years later.

But it says a great deal for the courage and determination of the particular divers that they lived with the image that haunted them. And managed to exorcise it through the ocean.

Down in the shark cage dipping in the swells in the dim-lit world below the dead whales at Albany we sometimes thought of these other incidents too. Wondered how it had been for those divers at other times. Thoughts flickering at random while we waited for *Carcharodon* to put his face into our camera gap with that deadly bottom-toothed grin. To catch us unaware again and make our stomach muscles contract like elastic bands going *snap*!

And of course, having the time, and the particular situation, we pondered the relationship of human and shark. And considered the reports we had studied of White Shark attacks—the epithets applied to sharks in newspaper and television reports were thought-provoking.

"Bloodthirsty killers," for example, was a description that could be applied to some of the many many humans who have committed unspeakable and "inhuman" deeds in crime or war. But in terms of the shark's role in the ocean, which we were beginning to understand, the labels seemed inappropriate.

There was an opposite view as well.

Those people who had seen from the safety of the surface the lithe beauty of the sharks, their smooth passage through the ocean, and their unhurried grace, deduced from this that they must be serene and "gentle" creatures. But they had also wandered from the path of reality into the world of fairy tales. To the realm of *Bambi* and *The Lion King*, those delightful but utterly unrealistic Walt Disney fantasies, in which animals think and talk like humans.

From our vantage point in the shark cage we could see that none of these human perspectives about sharks, ascribing "good" or "evil" qualities to them, were valid.

They were simply sharks and, like most other creatures in the sea, survival was the name of their game. Eat or be eaten. That was the truth of the matter.

The sharks showed us a side of Nature not many people have had the privilege of observing at close quarters. The Great Whites were elite beasts on the highest scale of predators. There was no question what they thought about us.

We were prey. It was as simple as that. And we were about to learn more on that aspect of life below the waves.

Shark Attack!

Bret Gilliam

Bret Gilliam is one of the world's foremost diving experts, and the current world record holder for depth diving on compressed air, at 464 feet. He may well have surpassed the then-existing record during his daring effort to save his partner from a fatal shark attack, as described in the following account, considered by many as one of the great adventure sagas of the twentieth century.

Rod Temple and Robbie McIlvaine were waiting for me when I drove up to the beach at Cane Bay on St. Croix's north shore. This area of the Virgin Islands had some of the best wall diving in the eastern Caribbean, and the drop-off was an easy swim from shore, eliminating the need for a long boat ride from Christiansted. We unloaded our gear and began to dress under the shade of the palms while a dozen or so tourists watched with interest. Diving was still not an everyday sport for most people, and the double tanks and underwater camera equipment held a certain fascination.

We were setting off to recover some samples from a collecting experiment we had placed on the wall for a local marine science lab. Six days earlier we had positioned our large support float right over the drop-off with the research vessel and carefully loaded our sediment traps, nets, and lines so they'd be ready for positioning in various locations in the shallow patch reef and the deep wall. Today we planned to inspect one project at 210 feet (64 meters) and shoot some photographs of the area. Rod transferred the dive profile and decompression information to his slate as Robbie and I rounded up the remainder of the equipment and walked into the warm ocean to begin our leisurely surface swim to the float station about 300 yards (270 meters) offshore.

We'd done Cane Bay hundreds of times in the previous two years, both for work and for fun, and this October morning was no different from scores of others as we snorkeled over the clear sand a few feet beneath our fins. As usual, Rod struck a livelier pace and forged on ahead while we wallowed in his wake, towing the photo gear and another Plexiglas sand trap the lab wanted set in the chute that spilled over the wall.

Reaching the float, Robbie retrieved the snap swivels that would anchor the trap into the rope grid we had strung on the wall face. Rod reviewed the deco schedule. "Look, if we can get this thing set up and check out the project at 210 in fifteen minutes, we can save a lot of decompression. Can you do the photos in that time frame if I run the lines on the Plexi trays?"

"Sure," I replied, "but don't go wandering off, in case Robbie needs help getting snapped in with the trap. That thing's a bitch to swim with."

"No problem." Rod smiled back. "I don't mind doing the heavy work for you lazy Yanks."

His British enthusiasm belied the fact that Robbie and I were about twice his size and strength, although he was older and more experienced. We both gave him an "up yours" salute, knowing full well that any heavy lifting always came our way while Rod handled the paperwork. As the timekeeper and dive leader, he would keep track of our dive profile, work in progress, remaining air status, and then run the deco schedule.

He eased away from the float and began to swim the short distance over the deep blue that marked the drop-off. The visibility was great, over 125 feet (38 meters) horizontally and even better looking up and down. A mild swell wrapped around the point and the sea was calm. Two of the Navy vessels that we worked with on submarine listening tests were just a few miles offshore and we could hear their acoustical sound-generators pinging away as we descended.

Rod settled in on top of the wall at 100 feet (30 meters) and we joined up to check gauges before slipping over in a gentle glide to the first workstation at 180 feet (55 meters). Robbie rearranged the open ends of the traps to aim in the west quadrant that week and I fired off photos to record the scene. Most scientists who contracted us didn't do much diving themselves and they insisted on reams of photographs so they could get an accurate idea of conditions in the deep-water zones they were studying.

Signaling that we were finished, Rod led us over the coral buttresses and came to rest next to the deep project. It had slid a bit deeper during the week, so Robbie and I eased it back into position and hoped it would stay put this time. This occupied our attention for most of ten minutes, after which Rod excitedly tapped me on the shoulder to point out the approach of two oceanic whitetip sharks. This was nothing new to us, as we dived with sharks routinely, but it was rare to see these open-ocean species in so close to shore. They passed within about 10 feet (3 meters) of us, and I shot a few photos as they swam off to the east.

We finished up the required observations and Rod filled out the field logs on his slate. Right on schedule he indicated, we were going to get out with only about twenty minutes deco, it looked like. Robbie started up first and pointed out the sharks again as they swam by him, headed over the coral and down into the sand chute. I remember thinking how strange it was to see oceanic whitetips right here on the wall at Cane Bay. It was kind of like walking off your back porch and seeing an African lion when you expected an alley cat.

We'd had our fair share of nasty encounters with whitetips when we worked offshore. They frequently bit our equipment, the steel cables deployed from the research vessel, and even the shafts and propellers on occasion. We were convinced that they would bite us as well once they got going, and never turned out backs on them without another diver riding shotgun. But these two didn't seem to pay any attention to us and I turned to begin the ascent behind Robbie.

Our plan called for Rod to be the last guy up. I rendezvoused with Robbie at about 175 feet (53 meters) just over a ledge and we both rested on the coral to wait for him to join us. He was late, and Robbie fidgeted, pointing to his pressure gauge, not wanting to run low on air. I shrugged and gave him a "What am I supposed to do?" look, and we continued to wait. Suddenly Robbie dropped his extra gear and catapulted himself toward the wall, pointing at a mass of bubble exhaust coming from the deeper water.

We both figured that Rod had experienced some sort of air failure at either the manifold of his doubles or his regulator. Since my air consumption was lower, I decided to send Robbie up and I would go to see if Rod needed help. As I descended into the bubble cloud, Robbie gave me an anxious okay sign and started up.

But when I reached Rod, things were about as bad as they could get. One of the sharks had bitten him on the left thigh, and blood was gushing in green clouds from the wound. I was horrified and couldn't believe my eyes. He was desperately trying to beat the 12-foot (3.6 meter) animal off his leg and to keep from sinking deeper. I had no idea where the second shark was and lunged to grab his right shoulder-harness strap to pull him up.

Almost simultaneously the second shark hit Rod in the same leg and bit him savagely. I could see Rod desperately gouging at the shark's eyes and gills as he grimly fought to beat off his attackers. With my free hand I blindly punched at the writhing torsos of the animals as they tore great hunks of flesh from my friend in flashes of open jaws and vicious teeth. Locked in mortal combat, we both beat at the sharks in a frantic panic. And then suddenly they let go and I dragged Rob up the sand chute, half walking and half swimming. Once clear of the silt, I could see Robbie about 100 feet (30 meters) above us, looking on in horror. He started down to us as I lifted Rod from the bottom and kicked with all my might toward the surface.

But in less than fifteen seconds the first shark returned and hit him again and began towing us both over the drop-off. The attack had probably lasted only a minute at this point, but Rod has lost a huge amount of blood and tissue and had gone limp in my grasp. I was still behind him, clutching his right harness strap, as the second larger shark hit him again on the opposite side, down around the left calf. Like the other, this shark bit and hung on as we tumbled down the wall face.

We were dropping rapidly, now completely out of control. My efforts to kick up were fruitless as the sharks continued to bite and tear at their victim, all the while dragging us deeper down. I felt Rod move again to fend off another attack and my hopes soared upon realizing that he was still alive. I clung briefly to the edge of the drop-off wall to arrest our rapid descent. The coral outcropping gave us some slight protection, and for a moment the attacks stopped.

Both sharks retreated into the blue and I watched them circle our position from about 10 feet (3 meters) away. To my horror I saw one shark swallow the remains of Rod's lower left leg. The other gulped a mouthful of flesh it had torn off. I tried to push Rod into the coral in an effort to shield him from another attack, but there was nothing that would afford any real shelter. As I turned away from the waiting predators, Rod and I came face to face for the first time during the attack. He shook his head weakly and tried to push me away. I grabbed his waist harness for a new grip and felt my hand sink into his mutilated torso. There was no harness left to reach for. He had been disemboweled.

Shrieking into my mouthpiece in fury, I pulled him from the coral and took off pumping for the surface clutching him to my chest. Immediately the sharks were on us again. I felt the larger one actually force me to one side as it savagely sought to return to the wounds that gushed billows of dark blood into the ocean around us. Rod screamed for the last time as the second shark seized him by the mid-section and shook him. The blue water turned horribly turbid with bits of human tissue and blood. Once we were turned completely over, and I felt Rod being torn away from me.

I watched his lifeless body drift into the abyss, with the sharks still hitting him. The attack had started at about 200 feet (60 meters). My depth gauge was pegged at 325 feet (99 meters) now, but I knew we were far deeper than that. The grimness of my own situation forced itself on me through a fog of narcosis and exhaustion.

That's when I ran out of air. I think that subconsciously I almost decided to stay there and die. The situation seemed so totally hopeless and my strength was completely sapped. But I put my head back and put all my muscle into a wide, steady power kick for the surface. I willed myself to maintain that kick cycle and forced myself upward.

After what seemed like an eternity, I sneaked a look at my depth gauge: it was still pegged at 325 feet. I sucked hard on the regulator and got a bit of breath. Not much, but it fueled my oxygen-starved brain a bit longer and I prayed my legs would get me up shallow enough to take another breath before the effects of hypoxia shut my system down forever.

There's really no way to describe what it's like to slowly starve the brain of oxygen in combination with adrenaline-induced survival instincts. But I remember thinking if I could just concentrate on kicking I could make it. After a while the sense of urgency faded and I remember looking for the surface through a red haze that gradually closed down to a tunnel before I passed out. The panic was gone and I went to sleep thinking "Damn, I almost made it."

I woke up on the surface, retching and expelling huge burps of expanding air. Apparently the small volume of air in the safety vest I wore had been enough to float me the final distance and save my life. But I still had to deal with an unknown amount of omitted decompression and the certainty that I was still severely bent.

Swimming to shore as fast as I could, I felt my legs go numb. By the time I reached the beach I could barely stand. A couple on their honeymoon waded out and dragged me up on the sand. I gasped out instructions to get the oxygen unit from our van, then collapsed. In an incredible burst of good fortune, it turned out the wife was an ER nurse from Florida and understood the pathology of decompression sickness. She and her husband got a steady flow of oxygen into me and ran to call the diving emergency numbers that were on the dive clipboard.

I drifted away again into unconsciousness and was revived at the airport, where a medevac flight was waiting to fly me to Puerto Rico. But the Navy chamber was down and it was decided that I would be taken to the only other functional facility, up on the island's northwest corner, nearly 200 miles (320 kilometers) farther away. But the flight crew was afraid I wouldn't make it when we ran low on oxygen shortly after passing San Juan. So they had the police stop traffic on the main divided highway and landed on the road, where a waiting Coast Guard helicopter sped me away to the hospital roof.

Two days later I was released but with residual numbness in my arms and legs, substantial hearing loss, and legal blindness in my right eye, which persists to this day.

Robbie's last view of Rod and me was as we were dragged over the wall in a cloud of blood by the sharks. He never saw my free ascent and so reported us both killed when he got to shore. It was not until the day I called my dad from the hospital that he knew I had survived. A week later we had Rod's memorial service at the beach. I resumed diving the next day. His body was never recovered.

EPILOGUE

This attack was widely reported, and shark experts speculate that the oceanic whitetips may have been attracted, and then stimulated, by the low-frequency sound in the water from the nearby submarine testing. The previous greatest depth from which a diver survived a free ascent was 180 feet (55 meters). Gilliam was probably closer to 400 feet (120 meters). He was cited for heroism by the Virgin Islands government for risking his own life to try to save his partner. In 1993, the British Broadcasting Corporation (BBC) produced a program about the incident as part of a series called *Dead Men's Tales.*

ACAPULCO

Lloyd Grove

There have been many documented fatal shark attacks off Acapulco's luxury hotel beaches. But official artistry in swindling the facts with doubletalk and plain hogwash has served to divert attention from the mutilated tourists who occasionally wash up on their beaches. Here, journalist Lloyd Grove ventures south of the border to get some hard answers about the story behind what Crawdaddy magazine called "the real Jaws."

Mid-morning on La Playa Revolcadero, southeast of Acapulco Bay, the air is already crammed with summer heat. Leonel and Nicholas, a native boy and his big-jawed and brawny companion, lounge atop their lifeguard stand in front of the Pierre Marques Hotel y Club de Golf, a pool-dotted oasis beyond an 8-foot-tall fieldstone embankment. Chatting and rubbing themselves with suntan oil, Leonel and Nicholas squint at the dull edge of the Pacific Coast not 30 feet away. Here, at 17° north latitude, where the ocean is a vast, unobstructed waterway to the Philippines, a prosperous-looking Mexican family—their blood doubtless more Spanish than Aztec, but red and thick nonetheless—thrashes happily in waist-high surf. In a sense, everyone here is lucky: Leonel and Nicholas, because they hold good jobs in a woefully depressed off-season economy, because their shiny bodies are healthy when many go sick and unattended; the family, because the chic young parents and their two giggling children are rich enough to jet from Mexico City to paradise in the middle of September—and because when the day is done, their fine Spanish blood has not spilled into Revolcadero's churning water.

The news, or suggestion, of shark attacks sends small shudders rippling through Acapulco, whose population of nearly 500,000 is all but completely dependent on tourism. Once a quiet fishing village, Acapulco emerged two decades ago as *the* playground for the wandering well-to-do. But the rapidly growing city, for all its cosmopolitan charm, was cursed with a nervous tic.

Today, sharks of several man-eating varieties come and go, swimming silently along the open beaches and within the deceptively bright-blue bay itself. (Actually, much of the city's raw sewage, along with waste and garbage from some of the finer hotels and restaurants, ends up in the bay—a situation that, despite warnings of stiff penalties for polluters, the government so far has been unable to correct.) Fishermen sometimes set out evenings for the open sea and return mornings in sturdy wooden launches piled high with 6-foot sharks. Walking along the bay one afternoon, I counted eight, their heads cut off, packed in the back of a pickup truck. Every so often a tourist gets mauled—or worse. Yet most of Acapulco's visitors seem too busy to take notice. More likely, they never suspect the danger.

"Such publicity would do very great harm to Acapulco," says Carlos Ortiz Ortiz, a street-wise journalist respected locally for his aggressive reporting on police corruption in a weekly tabloid called *2002*. According to Ortiz and others, members of Acapulco's all-important tourist industry—from hoteliers to policemen to cab drivers—routinely suppress reports of shark attacks. Such reports, Ortiz says, are relegated to back pages of the Spanish-language dailies, and rarely, if ever, appear in the English-language papers. "Of course it's a scandal," Ortiz concedes "but what can be done about it?"

"So far we've been very lucky," he says. "Most of the victims have been Mexicans."

For the promise of $300—tantamount to two months' salary at Acapulco's rarely enforced minimum wage of 125 pesos per day—Ortiz, a sometime stringer for the Associated Press, readily agreed to serve as legman for this story and to provide photographs of victims of shark attacks that occurred as recently as January 1977. After a month of daily phone contact, the pictures never materialized, and finally Ortiz stopped answering his telephone. One day I discovered the line had been disconnected.

"If I were you," said John E. Newman Jr., an Austin, Texas, lawyer who used to be a travel agent, "I wouldn't go down there and ask a lot of questions about sharks." Newman who regularly took groups of college students to Acapulco—during one such tour, a University of Texas student was raped by a cab driver and another was killed by a shark—went on: "It doesn't take much money to have somebody taken care of. . . . Don't laugh. They play by different rules down there."

On La Playa Revolcadero, a beach that takes its name from the Spanish verb *revolcar*—to knock down, to turn over and over, to flounder—sharks killed at least three tourists between December 1972 and April 1973. Two of the victims, an American doctor and a Canadian insurance executive, were swimming in waist-deep water directly in front of Pierre Marques, where they were guests. The other, a Canadian teenager, was body-surfing in front of the Princess, a great flower-draped pyramid of a hotel that looms about 500 yards down the beach. Like the Pierre Marques and eleven other hotels around the world, the Princess is owned by Princess Hotels International, Inc., in turn owned circuitously by American shipping baron Daniel K. Ludwig of New York. As in other cases, none of the victims was warned about sharks, although a small sign and red flag on each end of Revolcadero caution against a DANGEROUS UNDERTOW.

The evidence suggests that lifeguards and other hotel employees, perfectly aware of the presence of sharks, actually encouraged people to swim.

Monday afternoon, December 25, 1972, a shark picked seventeen-year-old Gerald Robbie Soukop of Vancouver, British Columbia, out of a group of body-surfers in front of the Princess. The shark struck in 4 feet of water, severing a hand and mutilating Soukop's right leg and torso. The boy bled to death on the beach. Soukop, however, was not a guest at the hotel, and the incident caused only a mild stir. "The lifeguards did nothing about keeping people out of the water after that," one guest wrote later to Henry H. Lipsig, a New York lawyer who was gathering information on the two subsequent deaths that became the basis for lawsuits. "The Princess Hotel did not notify newly arriving guests of the danger and the local newspapers did nothing by way of publicity. . . ."

Two months later, on Tuesday, February 27, 1973, Dr. Leo Ephraim Fischer, a fifty-seven-year-old orthopedic surgeon from Jersey City, strolled from his room at the Pierre Marques to Revolcadero. Fischer waded in and swam untroubled for several minutes before the shark appeared. It lunged at him repeatedly, savagely mangling his left arm, tearing away his left leg. The body floated off with the undertow, but hotel employees managed to reclaim it hours later. His widow, suing the Pierre Marques on a negligence charge, filed an affidavit with a New York state court. The day before Dr. Fischer's death, she said in her sworn statement, he had asked a lifeguard about the fins he saw in the water. The lifeguard had reportedly told him not to worry.

Five days after Dr. Fischer's death, a California businessman checked into the Pierre Marques and hiked at once to the beach. "Thinking in terms of water pollution," the man wrote the following August to Lipsig, "I was somewhat reluctant to swim, but in the absence of any warnings in the form of signs, lifeguards or notices from the management of any kind, I did swim. Fortunately, I looked toward the shore and noticed two guests running toward me gesticulating. . . ." Once they had waved him out of the water, the guests told the businessman about the deaths on the beach. It was the first he'd heard of the incidents.

Next month, Princess Hotels International, Inc. and the Mexican government talked privately about installing a kind of mesh nets that protect beaches along the shark-infested waters of Durban, South Africa. "We wanted to put them in," the manager of the Pierre Marques told Leslie Plommer, a reporter for the Toronto *Globe and Mail.* "The government wouldn't allow it." The hotel apparently wanted the government to underwrite half the cost; the government reasoned that if sharks broke through the nets, it, too, could be held legally responsible.

Weeks later, just after 6:00 P.M. on Wednesday, April 4, 1973, a crowd of guests and hotel employees were huddled on Revolcadero in front of the Pierre Marques. They were "very quiet and subdued," said one observer. "Some people, particularly women, were obviously quite shaken by what they had heard or seen." What they had witnessed was another Vancouver man, struggling in bloody, thigh-deep water, and screaming, "Shark! Shark!" John P. R. Nicolls, a forty-five-year-old insurance executive and father of six, was then drawn out to sea. His would-be rescuers saw three dorsal fins cruising along the breakers, so they did not swim after him. Two hours later, the body washed ashore in three parts.

Next week, Evan Atkinson, a reporter for the Vancouver *Sun* and a close friend of Nicolls, flew down on assignment. Atkinson, once a resident of Acapulco, befriended a young photographer who collected autopsy photos, uncovered other shark attacks, and met three uncommunicative fishermen who had lately been hired by the Pierre Marques to catch sharks. One day, Atkinson returned to his hotel room to find his notes stolen, but his billfold untouched. He heard that his photographer friend had been jailed. "I thought then that it was a good time to leave," he recalls.

Both the widows of Dr. Fischer and Nicolls brought suit against the Pierre Marques and Princess Hotels in American courts. After years of legal battles and hundreds of inches of bad publicity in the Canadian and American press, Ludwig's agents paid Mrs. Fischer $275,000 and Mrs. Nicolls $350,000.

"That's all been long forgotten," Carmen Ibarra, the Princess' publicist, says of the deaths, "but they did happen." There is a tiny flutter in her voice. "I'd have to tell you that, because you'd find out about them and then you wouldn't believe anything I said. It was the strangest thing, you know? For some reason, the natives had been dynamiting the fish!" Conversations about sharks tend quickly to move on to other things.

On the lifeguard stand on Revolcadero, Nicholas scratches his belly. "Sure my friend," he says with the easy bearing of a country club retainer, "the sharks were here once. They attacked a man on this beach maybe"—he pauses to consider, fixing his gaze on some vacant place in the water—"five years ago."

Young Leonel goes bug-eyed. "They did?" he gasps.

"Oh, yes," Nicholas says, smiling pleasantly at the boy's reaction. "Didn't you know? It was a very famous case." He waves his beefy right arm toward a murky place just beyond the first row of breakers. "The sharks took him *there*." He gives a lean account of the Nicolls incident. His enthusiasm for details wanes with each query.

"No, no, *señor*, the sharks left," Nicholas says finally. The smile is gone now; he rubs his chin. "There's no danger." Then, excusing himself, Nicholas bounds from his perch and heads toward the Pierre Marques, where, in my room that morning, a chambermaid had urged to get the most out of my vacation by swimming off the "beautiful beach."

Presently, a barefoot couple in swimsuits trudges across the burning sand from the hotel. Their uncertain progress betrays them as first-visit gringos; a doctor near the end of his residency and his assistant-buyer-for-Bloomingdale's fiancée. Their faces all guilt and resentment, they wave away dried-out women and stick-figure children who linger on the beach clamoring to sell them bright baskets, beaded necklaces and dead armadillos; ignore six wrinkled, bony men who strive to rent them six wrinkled, bony horses; and pause at two hand-lettered signs.

The signs, in English and Spanish, painted red and black, say, DAN-GEROUS UNDERTOW, adding, SWIM AT YOUR OWN RISK. They direct the reader to a small pennant flying atop the lifeguard stand. If the pennant is red, says the legend, don't swim, because the current is too strong. If the pennant is yellow, swim, but exercise caution. And if the pennant is green, swim. Since the episode five years ago, the lifeguard stand in front of the Pierre Marques has never flown anything but the red flag.

"We always have the warning flag out, we always keep it red." Javier Gomez, the Pierre's director of sales, explains in the brochure-lined office. "It means that the guests have to watch themselves and be careful." Asked about the possibility of sharks in the water, Gomez shrugs and smiles. "That's not for us to judge," he says pleasantly. "Didn't you see those signs on the beach," he continues, "that say the beach is federal property and the hotel is not responsible for anything that happens on the beach? The guests must exercise care." Indeed, as recently at 1975, the hotel placed ominously worded cards in all rooms, absolving itself of "acts on the beach." Three years later, the cards have disappeared.

On Revolcadero, the American couple approaches Leonel's life-guard stand, which supports an upended row of inflatable rafts for the use of hotel guests. The man—like his companion, flushed from an over-abundance of good weather, sweat dribbling from his Club Med mus-tache—catches Leonel's eye and gestures toward the breakers.

"Is it safe?" he asks grappling with the native tongue.

"Yes, *señor,*" Leonel replies, shrugging. "It's safe."

They continue down to the water's dull edge, but the man turns around on the meat of his tender-pink heel.

"What about . . . are there sharks?" he asks.

"No sharks, *señor,*" Leonel says, his bored grin exposing yellow teeth.

"Are you sure?"

Leonel laughs, "Well I haven't seen any today."

Maybe not today, but there have been less halcyon days in Acapulco.

On Sunday, August 23, 1964, Thad Moore of Alexandria, Virginia, was floating on his back in an inner tube about 150 yards off one of Acapulco's open beaches. He glanced to his right and, as he recalled later, "saw a dark shape swimming rapidly toward me. In a split second the shark hit my right thigh, knocking me out of the inner tube, with its snout across the top of my right leg. I struck the shark on the snout as hard as I could several times, and it let go suddenly and swam away quickly. The water turned red all around me and I knew I was injured seriously. . . . To my amazement, the shark never returned—this has been my greatest fear."

An animal described by (even) the Mexican press as "a huge shark" attacked a twenty-two-year-old American tourist on Saturday, January 10, 1970. Jack Kendall was swimming off La Playa Copacabana, adjoining the southeast end of Revolcadero. The creature shredded one of Kendall's legs before he was pulled into a passing motorboat. The previous Monday, another tourist had been hit in the bay, off La Playa Condesa, where American Airlines opened the Condesa Del Mar Hotel the following year. For a short time, swimming at both beaches was banned. An account in the *News of Mexico,* the English-language daily published in Mexico City, noted that local authorities "called upon the information media not to blow up the incidents since they could sharply reduce tourism, the mainstay of Acapulco's economy." Authorities further promised "to take adequate measures to protect swimmers."

Fifteen months later, a nineteen-year-old University of Texas student, Jimmy Rowe, on a tour called "Acapulco Adventures '71," accepted an invitation to surf off Copacabana. Tuesday morning, April 6, 1971, Rowe accompanied Ben Carter Katz, also part of the tour, and several others to the beach. Katz, a San Antonio land developer and Rowe's roommate at the Hotel Barracuda recalls: "We borrowed boards from two guys from Florida and arrived about nine. Before we even got in the water, one of the Florida guys said, "We can surf here till 11 o'clock, but we gotta get out at 11, because they start eating. The whole town dumps its sewage in the bay and when it starts floating out there, the sharks come in."

At the appointed hour the surfing party came ashore, but Rowe insisted on going out for another try. While he was paddling out about 100 yards from the beach, the shark struck. Its extended lower jaw caught his left thigh, cleanly severing the femoral artery. Katz swam in to get him. Rowe died in a rented jeep on the way to the hospital from—according to the official report—"acute loss of blood due to a wound produced by the bite of an animal." The word "shark" appears nowhere on the death certificate signed by Hermilio Arrieta Mateos of the civil registry.

As Rowe's body lay in an adjacent room at the Red Cross Hospital in downtown Acapulco, local police interrogated Katz. In fluent English, Katz insists, a police captain told him, "Before you say anything, I think you should know we have a law here. The law is that if you see something, it's your responsibility. . . . So you saw your friend surfing out there, and the surf was very strong, yes? And the surfboard slipped around and got him in the leg, yes?" Katz, dazed and frightened, agreed. Unable to move, he spent the next two days sequestered in his hotel room.

The tour leader, John Newman, then all of twenty-three, took charge of the body, arranging with the help of local restauranteur to have it kept in a food locker at the Paraiso Marriott Hotel on Acapulco's main drag. The American vice consul happened to be in town that day on his fortnightly visit from Mexico City (the United States, unlike nine other countries including the Netherlands and the Philippines, does not keep a permanent consulate in Acapulco). He did the paperwork that always accompanies a corpse on foreign soil. "He handled it like a stock transaction," Newman says. "He was like an executive—'Let's get it over with'— with no thought of the other person's feelings." In a conference room at the Marriott, the two argued bitterly over who would notify Rowe's parents. The vice consul, Newman says, was anxious to inform them so that he could return to Mexico City.

"We're in the diplomacy business," Claude Villarreal, the U.S. embassy's press attaché, explains six years later, "not the shark attack business."

Katz's horrors were not finished. He returned to Acapulco in December 1973, with a lady friend from San Antonio. Recurrent nightmares about Jimmy Rowe's death while swimming—"that instantaneous, camera-clicking moment," as Katz describes it—had finally ceased the year before. Until one afternoon in the second week of December, when Katz and his friend boarded the yacht, *Mexico Fiesta*, for a cruise around the bay. The three-deck steamer, filled with hundreds of revelers, pulled away from her downtown dock about 5:00 P.M., heading east. In the twenty minutes it took her to glide past the boot-shaped peninsula called "El Elefante," the party had warmed up considerably. On a dare, Katz says, a drunken American in his early twenties stripped to his underwear and jumped over the starboard side.

Almost immediately, the captain killed the engines, leaving the ship dead in the water. The jumper, treading water, drifted past the bow toward the gaping mouth of the bay. "About 200 yards off the bow, he started bouncing up and down with a violent jerking motion," says Katz's friend, who was standing at a railing in a crush of onlookers. "There were dark stains in the water. Not red, but black-looking." Crewmen went out in a dinghy and brought him back in a burlap bag. "They said it was a shark," she recalls, "and they made not another comment." Waving away questions from agitated tourists, the crewmen rushed into a cabin and locked the door.

Katz leaned over the railing. "I threw up. I kept throwing up," he says. "I just heaved and heaved and heaved. I couldn't believe it. I just cried like a baby."

One more for the record.

In the second week of January, 1977, a young Mexican decided to swim in the bay after drinking beer after beer on La Playa Hornos, a beach where Acapulcans enjoy spending afternoons with their families. "He should have known better," says a local reporter who covered the incident for *El Tropico,* one of the city's oldest daily newspapers. The man, never identified, dove into the filmy water about 2:30 P.M., the reporter says, and commenced a vigorous freestyle toward the open ocean. The sight of someone alone, so far out in the bay was unusual, and other Mexicans sitting on the beach began to watch. Twice they saw a dark fin surface near the swimmer, now more than 100 yards out. The second time the fin rushed on the swimmer, who was suddenly sucked below. The body washed ashore six hours later, missing the left leg and badly mangled in the neck. The victim was buried in a pauper's grave beyond the cliffs that ring the city.

At last count, Acapulco had nearly 400 hotels, 173 restaurants and ten discotheques for nearly four million vacationers each year—all this and more, the responsibility of Alejandro Gonzalez Molina, the city's thirty-one-year-old federal delegate of tourism. Alex Molina, as he calls himself, sets prices on menus, fixes parking tickets for foreign tourists, can even retrieve a confiscated license plate from the police.

"My forte," Alex Molina says, pronouncing the word in one syllable, "is promoting tourism." He is a pale man who rarely goes outside.

"To understand what is happening to tourism in Acapulco," he continues, popping a piece of hard candy into his mouth, "you have to go back three years. Up until 1974, there was a regular uprise, maybe 8–12 percent a year. But then in 1975, there was the economy crisis and the oil crisis in the States. And then," he sighs, "there was the Zionism boycott." He grins boyishly, the pencil mustache thinning out across his upper lip. "Oh boy, that gave us some headaches, let me tell you. . . ."

He stops for a question. "What? Sharks? That's not a problem here. There have been only one or two attacks in the ten years I've been here. All the beaches are safe, even the open beaches." He laughs softly, "You sure ask a lot of questions. Tell me, what are you writing about, anyway?"

"Well," he says, "there are hundreds of 'jaws' we have coming down from the north. Like everywhere, you find all kinds of sea animals. Whatever 'jaws' we have, they swim down from the north." He laughs again. "I mean the United States."

Gail Dorantes, whose name has been supplied by the embassy as a crack American journalist who has lived twenty years in Acapulco (she is a local stringer for United Press International), finishes lunch in the Sanborne's coffee shop downtown. "I'll be very frank," she says, blue bullets in her eyes. "I'm not going to help you at all because that's a dumb idea. That frank enough?" Her weathered smile starts to fade. "You think I'm crazy? Acapulco runs on tourism, tourism all the way, and as tourism goes, so go I." She stirs her iced tea, sips, then stirs again. "Really. That's the last thing we need. More people get killed by boat propellers anyway."

The parish of Rev. John Black, Acapulco's only full-time Episcopal priest, has served since 1964 as a clearinghouse for Americans in trouble. "I've never heard of any shark cases," the Rev. Black says flatly. "I always go on hospital tours, and I've never heard of any." He sips his milkshake (he says the sugar is good for a recent case of hepatitis). "Have you ever heard the expression, '¿Porque los pendejos y la mala suerte siempre andan juntos*" he goes on. "You know what pendejo means, don't you? You know, schlimazel. Think about it. Why is it that idiots [a polite translation] and bad luck always walk together?"

"There's a freedom here that you don't find in America," the Rev. Black says, "a laissez-faire environment. It's 'survival of the fittest,' call it that. Or, 'the greatest good for the greatest number.'"

Mike Oliver, the American expatriate editor of the Acapulco News, the city's English-language weekly, is nursing his fourth rum-and-Coke. "How often do they attack in the bay?" I ask.

"Oh, not too often."

"About two or three times a year? Once every four months?"

Oliver scrunches and unscrunches his face. "Yeah, that's about right," he says. "It's usually the same story. Some stupid broad is having her period but she just has to go swimming. A shark comes around and grabs her."

Acapulco is the richest city in the state of Guerrero—in turn, one of Mexico's poorest agricultural regions. Each year, desperately poor Mexicans arrive by the thousands in search of jobs; few find them. From 1970 to 1975, the years studied in a special government census, Acapulco's unemployment rate increased four-fold to about 15 percent But that figure accounted for less than half of the working-age population. The majority was not considered part of the workforce. Of those gainfully employed, 37 percent worked directly in the tourist industry, while the rest were in supporting industries like transportation and food production.

"There is much unemployment, but things will get better," says Manuel Pavon Bahaine, former head of the *Fideicomisa,* Acapulco's federal public works agency. Pavon Bahaine—along with Febronio Figueroa, nephew of Guerrero's governor and now Acapulco's mayor—sits in the marble-decked patio of one of the city's most spectacular villas overlooking the bay. Pavon Bahaine, sipping white wine, is describing a government project, his own idea, to turn the "Black Lagoon"—a heavily populated area between Revolcadero and the bay—into a multimillion dollar resort. His audience is Gail Dorantes; Dario Borzani, a prominent restauranteur from Mexico City; Baron Felipe Houseman, a gentleman of leisure with a perpetually sardonic smile, and me. Three dark-suited bodyguards, brought by Pavon Bahaine and Figueroa, linger at the bar. Figueroa, meanwhile, takes off his shirt to show a bikini-clad travel reporter for a Spanish magazine an old war wound (four years ago, he and his uncle, Ruben Figueroa Figueroa, were kidnapped by Mexican revolutionaries; they escaped in a fearsome gunfight near the city). Jacqueline Petit, Acapulco's premier hostess and owner of the villa is busy nearby placing a call to an ocean liner docked in the bay. "I must get Elke Sommer to lunch," Jacqueline says breathlessly. "She's so much fun."

I broach the unpleasant subject to Pavon Bahaine. Everyone listens. Baron Houseman looks sourly amused. "Where the beaches are more open to the ocean," Pavon Bahaine explains, "it's not a good idea to swim. There's no protection. Of course there are no nets anywhere."

Borzani interrupts in a voice that is almost a wail. "I already told you," he cries, "only careless people swim off those beaches. People know not to swim off those beaches—that's crazy," while Figueroa, for the benefit of the Spanish reporter, adds with a shrug, "The bay is completely safe. I swim there all the time, and there are absolutely no sharks."

There is an awkward silence while Gail Dorantes fidgets with a necklace and Jacqueline Petit plays with a telephone dial. Pavon Bahaine chuckles.

"The only sharks who come into Acapulco," he says, slapping his knee, "are us."

The Great Shark of Jurien Bay

Hugh Edwards

With half of his diving partner's body inside a shark's gullet, who could have faulted Lee if he had swum off for his life. Instead, Lee sucked down a breath and dove toward the fray with his spear gun, hell-bent on interrupting the attack. Insane? Fatalistic? In fact, such courageous acts are repeatedly found in the shark attack literature. It's as if the predator triggers the boldness of everyone in its orbit.

On August 19, 1967, two spearfishermen swam seawards from the limestone bluff of North Head at Jurien Bay, a remote spot on the coast of Western Australia.

Their names were Robert Bartle and Lee Warner. Both men were clad in the black neoprene rubber suits with hoods that were standard among divers at the time. Their full face masks glinted in the pale August sun. Bartle had on a short suit, cut off at the knees, a factor which may have had some later significance. Warner wore a full suit, for the water still had a winter chill about it, together with the green-yellow tinge and poor visibility that went with the time of year. Clear blue water and the warmth of the Leeuwin Current would come with early summer. But that was still two months away.

The divers were heading toward some reefs marked by the white spray of breakers more than a kilometer offshore. They swam with their powerful single-rubber spear guns held out in front of them and with the steady, economical fin strokes that eat up distance. Glancing back from time to time to check their distance from the shore, they could see the vehicles parked at random angles on the scrub-covered heights above the gray headland. Bartle's Volkswagen, with its familiar beetle shape, was among them.

The two swimmers were contrasts in physique and personality. Bob Bartle was a pleasant-faced fellow, twenty-four years old, short but strongly built. He worked hard in his family's hardware business but in his spare time he lived, breathed, and dreamed diving. A natural organizer, he was secretary of the Western Australian Council of Underwater Activities.

Lee Warner was twenty-six, a former school teacher who had taken time off from the classroom to pursue his passion for underwater sport. Warner had an impressive natural physique, piercing blue eyes, and a black bushy beard. He had a devil-may-care attitude to life, casual and carefree. But he was very serious about his diving. He could free-dive on a breath to 30 meters (100 feet).

Each man towed a float with a blue and white diver's flag at the end of a long cord. The floats were dual-purpose. The flag warned boats of the diver's position, and wire toggles hung from the float to hold the fish he had speared. To left and right of Warner and Bartle other flags moved out to sea. They were towed by divers from the other vehicles on the headland. They would be their opposition in the spearfishing competition to be held on the following day, Sunday, August 20.

This day, the Saturday, was scheduled as a practice day. Divers entered in the competition had come 240 kilometers north from Perth for the event. Now they had the opportunity to swim over ground, to note the underwater terrain, and hope that the fish they saw would still be there on the morrow when points would be scored for their catch. Not all the divers took the practice swim seriously. But Warner and Bartle had a strong sense of purpose. They were working to a long-term plan which included contesting the State Pairs Championships later in the year and the Australian Championships early in the new year of 1968.

The regular competitions held throughout the year were not especially important in the overall scheme of things. But, as every athlete knows, there is no practice like an actual contest. Warner and Bartle were hardening their bodies and sharpening their skills for the more important events ahead.

Warner was the more brilliant diver of the two. But Bartle had endurance and determination. Together they made an excellent combination as a pairs team. By August 1967 they had made hundreds of dives together and were among the top echelon of Australian spearfishermen.

None of the divers swimming at Jurien Bay used SCUBA because it was outside the rules. In competition, spearfisherman had to dive holding their breath. Some of the top Australian divers could take fish at 25 to 30 meters below the surface. But it took long practice, skill and a certain courage to reach those depths. The water at Jurien Bay, inside the reef, would be comparatively shallow. But breath-holding "blackout," a sometimes fatal affliction among competition divers, could occur in shallow waters as well as in the deeps.

In the distance the smooth winter swell broke with a sullen booming sound. There were distant feathers of spray on the outside reefs, the mist of the breakers hanging on the air. It was a light hazy day with a promise of spring about it. But down below the silver surface the surges restlessly sweeping the kelpweed showed that winter still held a grip.

The ground was barren some distance from shore. But the divers noted the positions of smaller fish such as red morwong, scaly-fin, silver drummer and zebra fish. Nothing much to cause excitement there.

What every spearfisherman hoped to see that day was jewfish. The Western Australian jewfish is a silver-scaled sea perch. Occasional specimens grow to 30 kilograms but they are more commonly seen at from 5 to 20 kilos. They are the State's premium table fish and a prestigious catch. Jewfish are most often found in caves and reef gullies with sandy bottoms. Underwater they have a characteristic black vee stripe across their heads which fades when the fish is taken from the water.

Warner and Bartle were seeking jewfish ground, and their thoughts were on finding broken country in the limestone reef bottom with holes and caves. Neither they nor any of the other divers had been concerned about sharks when they entered the water and the thought did not trouble them as they swam.

Both had had shark experiences. As a youth Warner had shot gray nurse sharks and some whalers and sold them to fish and chip shops for pocket money. The fish shops presented the fillets fried in batter as "snapper" or "kingfish." Shark actually tasted fine but the customers (who mostly knew what they were geting) preferred it under another name. With shark, you never knew what it had eaten!

Bartle had had to fight off an aggressive bronze whaler shark at Dunsborough earlier in the year, jabbing it away with his spear gun as it charged him repeatedly.

"If anyone asks me if I'm scared of sharks I wouldn't shrug my shoulders after Dunsborough," was his comment afterwards.

But the expert opinion at the time was that the danger of sharks was high only in summer. Statistics seemed to show that it was warm water and high temperatures which triggered attacks. Jurien Bay, in Western Australia's temperate zone, was cold in August. No question about that. "Cold enough to freeze the balls off a brass monkey," the first divers on the day reported, making wry faces as they walked into the water. Rough diving talk was a part of the camaraderie of competition.

In nearly twenty years of diving there had never been a fatal shark attack on a spearfisherman in Western Australia. It was not something that was regarded as a matter of concern. In eastern Australia, where there was a different record, boats patrolled vigilantly while spearfishing competitions were being held. But at Jurien Bay there were no boats because there seemed to be no need.

About 700 meters from the shore Bob Bartle gestured ahead with his spear gun and Lee Warner, swimming beside him, saw a hint of white sand in the distance. As they came closer they saw a depression in the seabed. It was a sunken sandy saucer, a hollow some 12 meters across, in about 8 meters of water with overhanging ledges.

Jewfish are nocturnal and often hole up under ledges during the day. The spot seemed barren of other fish species. But it was the kind of place where a jewfish might be hovering on silvery fins in the darkness under the overhangs.

"Better have a look," said Bob.

"Right oh."

There was a routine procedure. Bartle glided down in a shallow dive to peer under the ledges, dropping the lead anchor weight of his float as he did so, for greater freedom of movement.

Warner watched from above. Sometimes jewfish which had hidden came out from curiosity to look at the silver flash of the anchor weight, or followed a spearfisherman up after a dive. On a lucky day there might be two or more in a cave to share. But the second diver had to be quick because companion fish tended to "spook" after the first shot. Warner watched closely.

Bob examined the caves, disappearing at times under the ledges, but making a final "negative" sideways sign with his hand as he began to ascend. No jewfish. Well, that was not totally unexpected. They would have to look at the reefs further out as they had intended. Warner turned to swim on while Bartle dived again to retrieve his float weight.

Suddenly, and without warning, a huge dark shape hurtled under Warner's fins. It was so big and moving so fast, that he cried out involuntarily: "What the bloody hell. . . . !"

Without slackening speed the creature—Warner had not yet identified it as a shark—struck Bartle with tremendous force. The impact was so severe that his mask was dislodged. Then Bartle was seized between the hip and shoulder and shaken violently, like a dog shaking a rabbit.

Watching from above, Warner was frozen with horror. The attack was so sudden, so totally unexpected, that for a moment he could not grasp the reality of it. At that point, his eyes wide in shock, everything appeared to him to be happening in slow motion. The period of frozen immobility, of indecision, probably lasted only a few moments. To Lee Warner it seemed an eternity. But the discipline of years of diving rapidly returned and Warner saw what he had to do.

With his spear gun held in front of him, he filled his lungs with a deep breath and began his dive toward the struggling forms, that nightmare scene, below him.

He had killed sharks before and knew the vital spot behind the eyes. A spear piercing the brain there could kill any ordinary shark. He had never seen—or even imagined—a beast of this size before. But there was still a chance he might kill or immobilize it. Or at the very least distract it from its deadly purpose. In any case there was no option—apart from fleeing and leaving Bob Bartle to his fate, and that was unthinkable.

Bartle was still gripped in the jaws, dwarfed by the huge bulk of the creature which continued shaking him mercilessly from side to side.

Warner closed to firing range and took aim. Then he squeezed the trigger. The gun bucked in his hand and the stainless steel spear thudded home.

"I fired the spear into the top of the shark's head, where I figured the brain should be. It hit with a solid clunk, but it didn't seem to affect the shark. Except that it attracted its attention to me. It sort of shook its head and then rose up towards me."

As the monster angled up towards the surface it bit Bartle completely in half.

Warner gagged in horror as a cloud of blood welled upwards. Then the shark came up through the blood straight towards him.

In its mouth it still gripped the lower parrot of Bob Bartle, his fins protruding.

"Christ!" Warner screamed, eyes bulging behind his mask. "Jesus Christ Almighty!"

As the shark closed he pushed it away desperately with his unloaded spear gun. Jabbing at the great black eye.

A detached part of his mind noted that the eye rolled white. "I didn't think sharks could do that," he would say later. Then he was back to stark reality. The water was murked with blood. Shapes were distorted, grotesque in the darkened twilight sea. The huge shadow of the shark moved through it all.

"Never in my life have I seen anything so chilling as watching that shark circling around me with the body of Bob still in its jaws. From less than a meter away I could see the terrible wounds which had been inflicted. I felt helpless. I could see Bob was dead. That was only too obvious. I though I was soon to follow. I simply cannot describe the terror which flowed through me."

The shark continued to swim around him.

"It kept circling about 3 meters from me. Its body looked about 5 feet [1.5 meters] thick from top to bottom. I didn't really get a good idea of its length—I couldn't see its extremities and I don't remember seeing the tail. All I could see was the eye and what it had in its mouth."

Then his gaze was attracted to something else. "Out of the corner of my eye I saw Bob's gun which was still loaded and floating just below the surface. I grabbed it thinking, here was another chance! Swinging it around I tried to belt the spear into the shark's eye.

"But the eye was set close to the top of its head and somehow the spear just whistled over it and missed everything. It was the worst shot of my life. I don't know how I could have missed a target of that size and I've cursed myself for it a thousand times since.

"It was my last real chance to get back at the shark."

Now the shark was tangling the float and spear lines and there was a new danger.

"It kept circling round and round. It was tied to my gun from the first spear and the gun picked up the float lines and the line from Bob's gun. It all was just one big tangled mess.

"I was afraid of getting caught up in the lines myself.

"The shark was black on top, white on its guts, a sort of mottled pattern. It looked weird in the bad winter light and the blood-reddened water. The jaw looked wider than the body. It seemed at least a meter across. Maybe more.

"I knew Bob was dead, and then there was the thought of other sharks. A little bronze whaler came and began darting around in the blood. I wondered whether there were any more big ones. . . ."

Warner had no gun now, and no defenses of any kind. He began to swim backwards, breaking away from the shark.

"I felt pretty bloody helpless, I can tell you. I swam backwards at first, FAST. Looking back I could see the shark still swimming around tangled in the lines and floats at the same spot. Once I lost sight of it I began freestyling for shore. Now and again I looked back to convince myself that the shark wasn't following. I was still frightened.

"It wasn't too far to shore, but it seemed miles. I swam away from a friend and diving companion of seven years. Now that's something I'll never forget. Not as long as I live."

He ran stumbling from the water and looking back saw the flags of other divers out in the water, the swimmers still unaware of what had happened. He knew that he had to get help, and fast. Had to find someone with a boat to get the other divers out of the water.

It all seemed unreal—in fact the sense of nightmarish unreality never left him. It was such a short time since he and Bob had walked down to the water's edge with their fins and guns and gear. Laughing and joking, kidding each other about the cold swim.

Now that time seemed a whole world away.

Up on the bluff of North Head, his breath coming in gasps, Lee Warner searched frantically for the keys to Bob Bartle's Volkswagen. And could not find them. But he did find a key to one of the other cars. It started at the first turn of the key. "Thank God for that!" Then he drove skidding around corners on the gravel road, at breakneck speed, and kicking up fishtails of dirt on the turns. Heading toward the little fishing settlement at Sandy Cape, 10 kilometers away.

The fishing season was over but there were still a few boats in the anchorage. Some of the fishermen were relaxing, having a Saturday afternoon beer and listening to the football on the radio. Their peace was shattered at the sound of an approaching vehicle driven by an apparently crazy man. "Who the hell . . . ?"

Warner skidded to a halt and gasped out his story.

"Got to get them out of the water." His face showed the urgency. "Those other blokes. They don't know what's out there!"

The fishermen understood at once. They put their beers down. "What about your boat, Harry?"

"Let's get going, then!" said Harry Holmes. He was skipper of a 13.5 meter steel rock lobster boat *Gay Jan*, the most suitable boat in the bay. They all ran to his dinghy on the beach and in a short time the *Gay Jan* was off on her way to North Head at full throttle, exhausts blowing black diesel smoke. Soon she was rolling in the swell and picking up divers off the headland.

"Get out of the water, quick! There's been a shark attack!"

"Shark? Where . . . ? Who . . . ?"

Some of the divers were incredulous, finding it hard to believe. Until they saw Lee Warner's eyes.

A little later they saw something else.

The floats were still there, still attached by the tangled lines, the dark shape of the giant shark swimming beneath them.

There was also another object floating. When they brought the *Gay Jan* alongside the floating torso of Robert Bartle, some of the divers choked with nausea and could not look. The body was cut clean through the breastbone by one tremendous bite. Strangely enough the expression on Bob's face was peaceful, as though he had simply drifted off to sleep. His lungs were still filled with air, which showed he had not even cried out.

Death must have been very quick. It is possible that he was never aware of what had happened to him. His friends always hoped so in the aftermath.

Those aboard the *Gay Jan* caught hold of the lines and floats and tried to draw the shark in. But it was incredibly strong. As it began to swim away the lines snapped one by one, the metal fittings on the spears straightened and broke. Then it was gone. The shadow disappeared.

The divers held a wake that night at the Jurien Bay Hotel, drowning their sorrow in the traditional way. Some of them wept. Next day they held their spearfishing competition as scheduled. Their thoughts as they entered the water may be imagined. But they explained the reason: "Bob would have wanted it that way."

On that Sunday, August 20, 1967, the news was on the radio, Statewide. Like every other diver who had been in the Indian Ocean that weekend I asked myself the same question: "What if it had been me?" I had known Bob Bartle well. Lee Warner too.

There were other questions to be answered. I knew I would be going north to Jurien Bay the following day.

It was a road that would take me to other places as well. A long and winding trail following *Carcharodon carcharias*, the Great White shark.

Malevolent man-eater, or simply misunderstood? That was something I hoped one day to find out.

CLOSE ENCOUNTER

Joe Jackson

Imagining yourself in free diver Joe Jackson's wet suit during his face-to-face rendezvous with a Great White shark is an electrifying drill. One can only wonder, in all of history, how many other human beings have communicated with a Great White in its own liquid space and on its own instinctual wavelength.

In my dream I am facing a shark, hands on the stock of my spear gun, preparing to jab at him if he approaches nearer. I don't wish to injure or provoke it, but if it comes any closer I will have no choice. There is part of me that doesn't think, but simply knows somehow that I cannot give ground. It is an odd dream, with its central debate on how assertive I should be with a creature so much larger and more powerful than me. Perhaps less odd given I had gone to sleep pondering whether or not I would shoot at an approaching shark, as a fellow free diver had been forced to do in Mexico a year earlier. In the event, however, it would prove not to be a relevant question.

Seth Hopkins and I had been diving together a lot that summer. We had met on an abalone trip up near Mendocino over Memorial Day, and had made a couple of trips with others south to the Big Sur and up to the North Coast. Recently, we had taken to diving closer to home, in San Mateo County, and had found some good diving, despite the area's reputation for murky water and for being a bit sharky. Two weeks earlier at a local beach, we had together brought up a thirty-pound halibut from 40 feet of water with no floatline, a bit of a trick since I had aimed badly, and the minimally impaired fish seemed determined and able to pull either of us down after it.

This day found us diving off Fitzgerald Marine Preserve, a preserve mostly for mollusks, since spearfishing was expressly permitted. We suited up at the car and carried our gear. As we came down the path to the water, we met two other free divers exiting, an event unusual enough in itself (I had never seen another diver here), made more so by the fact that each carried a lingcod he had speared. Seth and I entered the water and kicked through the shallows, negotiating the breaking surf and urchin-covered ledge which marks the boundary of the preserve, and entered the open sea. The day was sunny and calm, the water almost glassy, with only the smallest of ripples sparkling in the sun.

Though I expected to come home with a fish or two for dinner, hunting was not my main priority: it was almost just an excuse to get in the water. The main draw was simply to be in that environment, to enter it deeply and become as much one with it as possible. Free diving offers a rare opportunity to synchronize the inner with the outer. It requires the diver to empty the mind of clutter, as surely as it requires filling the lungs with air. Failure to do either leads only to short dives and frustration. But when it all comes together, the requisite inner calm combines with the shift in environment and physical sensation to produce a change in consciousness so profound that entry into another world has as much a psychic and spiritual color to the meaning as physical. To slide beneath the surface of the sea is also to move into a deeper, quieter world. One can experience the sensual richness, wildness, and mystery of nature on its own terms, and the physiological correlates of breath-hold diving serve to deepen the connection. It is for this that I return, again and again.

So I had brought my spear gun along, but hadn't strung the power bands yet. The spear shaft was in place, but the gun was essentially unloaded. For safety reasons, this is my preferred method of carry when diving in close proximity to another diver. I planned to draw the power bands only toward the end of the dive, so I could get some fish but not have to trail their bleeding corpses along behind me for most of the dive. Seth was carrying a 3-inch-bladed dive knife.

Despite the relatively small waves, the water was somewhat murky, with only 8–10 feet of horizontal visibility at most, and we continued to gradually work our way out toward deeper and—we hoped—clearer water. As we moved along, we slipped into our regular diving pattern of resting together on the surface and breathing up, before exchanging wordless ready signals and commencing a dive. We were now in perhaps 35 or 40 feet of water and half a mile offshore. Seth tipped over and began finning down, the long blades propelling him with an easy grace into the deeper green below us. I took a final breath and followed him, spear gun gripped casually in my right hand. As I reached mid-water, I perceived a whitish streak at the right hand periphery of my vision, at about my level.

I thought momentarily it could be a rock ledge or a pinnacle reflecting light at me, though I wasn't aware of any that high in this area. As I turned my head toward it, I perceived first that it was moving, second that it was large, and finally that it was the back half of a Great White shark. The light-colored streak had been a glimpse of its white underside. It was "cutting the corner," slightly below me now, passing diagonally from my right and behind me to ahead and to the left of me. Descending like a ghost, it was vectoring in on where I knew Seth to be below, though my attention was now fully occupied by the apparitional creature. I ceased finning but continued my glide downward as momentum carried me to the level of the shark, which veered upward, as though suddenly becoming attuned to my presence. Now, hanging suspended only a few feet away, the full size and power of the beast was mind altering. A sensation of hyper-reality overtook me, putting the world into that timeless stop-action of dreams and extremity. The Great White was 12, perhaps 14 feet long, and as thick and solid looking as a redwood tree. But as it slowly turned toward me, there was a fluidity and power and presence unlike anything I had ever encountered. I had a moment of thinking, wondering, if this was going to be bad; if this was how it was just before it got very bad. Though I remained physiologically calm, mentally I wavered on the edge of panic. Then some instinct in me took over and there was no more thought, only the shark and I and a very small space between.

I raised my spear and pointed it at the shark, holding it not by the pistol grip as you would for shooting, but by the stock, poised to thrust or block. The shark's demeanor was beyond merely inquisitive. As it turned toward me, I faced it squarely and put the tip of the spear toward its face, now inches from my spear tip, trying to dissuade its closer approach without actually jabbing it. As its head veered away, I tried to lead the dance subtly by making a fraction of a kick, fading slightly along-side the silently languid beast. I had two purposes: one was to give the shark a little less room than it wanted to turn completely around toward me—I did not want to confront it head on. The other was to keep it in sight—I was terrified of not knowing where it was, of being suspended in mid-water, seeing only a short distance in any direction around me before vision faded into green haze, expecting an attack at every moment but not knowing from what quarter; vulnerable on all sides, and above, and below.

The ballet continued: the approach, the meeting, the turning away, three or four times more. Stark fear and an incredible sense of awe simultaneously flooded my being. Minute details became engrossingly clear—the lovely intermixing of white and brown on the shark's flank, powerful muscle rippling beneath smooth skin, and the gentle pulsation of the gill slits as the water flowed through them. It seemed I was doing the right things, presenting an alert but unfearful appearance to my "friend," but at every moment I was aware that if it came down to it, if the shark determined to attack, there was really very little I could do. The sharpened stick in my hands was badly overmatched against the power and momentum it so easily demonstrated with each effortless movement.

Again, another approach. Again, I held my ground, awaiting the worst. Then, finally, I saw the shark give a rapid, more definitive sweep of its tail and fade into the bright gloom. I began to gradually rise in the water, floating up slowly, not kicking, gazing intently but seeing only the late afternoon sunlight, washed green in the now empty sea, and the ghost-image left in my mind by the sharp V of the disappearing caudal fin.

Seth and I met up on the surface—he had viewed the encounter from the rocks below, silhouettes pirouetting a few feet above. "Load your gun!" (Thanks for the tip, Seth.) I already had one band cocked by the time he finished saying it, though it took my nervous fingers a few more agonizing seconds to finish the second one.

We paired up, shoulder to shoulder, and began slowly kicking toward shore. It was a long swim in, scanning all directions below and occasionally on the surface. We didn't stop to look for any lingcod. I was glad to have a reliable buddy at my side, so each of us only had to cover half of the attack angles below us.

A couple of times we lost shoulder contact for a few moments, then scared each other silly by colliding back together. I had a moment of terror as a dark shape loomed up from below me, but it was only a rocky pinnacle marking our approach to shallower water. I began to feel safer as we got into waist deep water, but didn't really relax until we were again on the beach, at which point we both collapsed, sitting on the beach and yakking at each other like a couple of nervously relieved seals, which is basically what we were.

I still enjoy diving frequently, and generally feel pretty relaxed in the water, but must admit that I haven't again dived at that particular spot with any feeling of security. Also, the distance which I will willingly swim before deciding that a kayak might be a better choice has shrunk considerably. Anything even remotely off shore now requires a boat nearby.

As I think back on the encounter from time to time, it is with a mixture of feelings. Given a hypothetical opportunity to again meet a Great White in open water with no protection, I don't know if I would take it, but at the same time, I would not have missed the experience for anything in the world. It remains the most intense and mystical experience of the sea I have ever had.

ATTACKED BY A KILLER SHARK!

Rodney Fox

Rodney Fox, champion Australian free diver and later a champion for the preservation of sharks, survived one of the grisliest shark attacks in history. His personal account of the ordeal is one of the great survival stories of all time.

ay looked miserable standing there as I said goodbye at 6:30 that Sunday morning in December 1963. She was expecting our first child, and the doctor had told her firmly: don't go.

I wish now that the doctor's advice had applied to me as well. Two hours later, however, found me standing on the cliff at Aldinga Beach, 34 miles south of our home in Adelaide, South Australia. Given my early start, I had time to study carefully the dark patterns of bottom growth on the coral reef that shelves to seaward under the incoming blue-green swells.

Aldinga reef is a teeming sea jungle and happy hunting ground for underwater spearfishermen like myself. Forty of us were waiting for the referee's 9:00 whistle to announce that the annual South Australian Skin Diving and Spearfishing Championship competition had begun. Each of us would have five hours to bring in to the judges the biggest bag, reckoned both by total weight and by number of different species of fish.

My own chances looked good. I had taken the 1961–62 championship and had been runner-up the following season. I had promised Kay that this would be my last competition. I meant to clinch the title and retire a winner, diving thenceforth only for fun, when Kay and I both might want to. I was twenty-three and after months of training, at peak of form. We were "free divers," using only wet suits, fins, face masks, snorkels, weight belts, and spearfishing guns. No SCUBA tanks allowed. I had trained myself to dive safely to 100 feet and to hold my breath for more than a minute without discomfort. At the 9:00 A.M. whistle blast we waded into the surf.

By way of a light line tied to our lead weight-belts, each man towed behind him a buoyant, hollow fish float. We would load our fish into these floats immediately after spearing them. This would minimize the amount of fresh blood released in the water. Blood might attract from out beyond the reef the big hunting fish—the always ravenous and lethal predatory sharks that prowl the deeper water off the South Australian coast. Lesser sharks—like the bronze whaler and gray nurse—are familiar to skin divers and have not proved aggressive. Fortunately the dread white hunter, or "white death" sharks, caught by professional fishermen in the open ocean, are rarely encountered by skin divers. But as a precaution two high-powered patrol boats crisscrossed our hunting area, keeping a wary lookout.

The weather was bright and hot. An offshore breeze flattened the green wave tops, but it roiled the water on the reef. Visibility under the surface would be poor, making it difficult for us to zero in on potential game. In murky water a diver often gets too close to a fish before he realizes that it's there; thus he scares it away before he can get set for a clean shot.

By 12:30, when I towed to shore a heavy catch of parrot fish, snapper, snook, boarfish, and magpie perch. I could see from the other piles that I was well up in the competition. I had sixty pounds of fish on shore, comprising fourteen species. It was now 12:35, and the contest was closed at 2:00. As fish naturally grew scarcer in the inshore areas I had ranged out to three quarters of a mile for bigger and better game. On my last swim-in from the "drop off" section of the reef, where it plunges from 25-foot to 60-foot depth, I had spotted quite a few large fish near a big triangular-shaped rock that I felt sure I could find again.

Two of these fish were dusky worwongs—or "strongfish," as Australian skin divers usually call them. Either of these would be large enough to tip the scales in my favor; then one more fish of another variety would sew things up for me. I swam out to the spot I'd picked, then rested face down, breathing through my snorkel as I studied through my face mask the best approach to two fish sheltering behind the rock. After several deep breaths I held one, swallowed to lock it in, up-ended and dived.

Swimming down and forward, so as not to spook them, I rounded the large rock and thrilled to see my quarry. Not 30 feet away the larger dusky morwong, a beauty of at least 20 pounds, was browsing in a clump of brown weed.

I glided forward, hoping for a close-in shot. I stretched both hands out in front of me, my left for balance, my right holding the gun, which was loaded with a stainless-steel shaft and barb. I drifted easily over the short weed and should have lined up for a perfect head-and-gill shot, but . . .

How can I describe the sudden silence? It was a perceptible *hush*, even in that quiet world, a motionlessness that was somehow communicable deep below the surface of the sea. Then something huge hit me with tremendous force on my left side, knocking my spear gun violently from my hand and ripping away my face mask. Heaved through the water at wild speed, I could see nothing in the blur.

I felt a bewildering sensation of nausea. The pressure on my back and chest was immense. A queer "cushiony" feeling ran down my right side, as if my insides on my left were being squeezed over to my right side.

The pressure on my body was choking me. Stunned senseless, I had no idea what was happening. I tried to shake myself loose but found that my body was clamped as if in a vise. With awful revulsion my mind came into focus, and I realized my predicament: *a shark had me in his jaws.*

I could not see the creature, but it had to be a huge one. Its teeth had closed around my chest and back, with my left shoulder forced into its throat. I was being thrust face down ahead of it as we raced through the water.

Although dazed with the horror, I felt no pain. In fact, there was no sharp feeling at all except for the crushing pressure on my back and chest. I stretched my arms out behind and groped for the monster's head, hoping to gouge its eyes.

Suddenly, miraculously, the pressure was gone from my chest. The creature had relaxed its jaws. I thrust backward to push myself away—but my right arm went straight into the shark's mouth.

Now I felt pain such as I had never imagined. Blinding bursts of agony made every part of my body scream in torment. As I wrenched my arm loose from the shark's jagged teeth, all-encompassing waves of pain swept through me. But I had succeeded in freeing myself.

I thrashed and kicked my way to the surface, thudding repeatedly into the shark's body. Finally my head pushed above water and I gulped great gasps of air. I knew the shark would come up for me. A fin brushed my flippers and then my knees suddenly touched its rough side. I grabbed with both arms, wrapping my arms and legs around the monster, hoping wildly that this maneuver would keep me out of his jaws. Somehow I gulped a great breath.

We went down again, so deep that I scraped the rocks on the bottom. Now I was shaken violently from side to side. I pushed away with all my remaining strength. I had to get back to the surface.

Once again I could breathe. But all around, the water was crimson with blood—my blood. The shark breached the surface a few feet away and turned over on its side. Its hideous body resembled a great rolling tree trunk, rust-colored, with huge pectoral fins. The great conical head belonged unmistakably to a white hunter. Here was the white-death itself!

It began moving toward me. Indescribable terror surged through my body. This fearful monster, this scavenger of the sea, was my master. I was alone in its domain; here the shark made the rules. I was no longer an Adelaide insurance salesman, rather a maimed and squirming meal, to be forgotten even before it was digested.

I knew the shark was attacking again and that I would die in agony when it struck. I could only wait. I breathed a hurried little prayer for Kay and the baby.

Then, in awe and disbelief, I saw the creature veer away just before it reached me, the slanted dorsal fin curving off just above the surface. The monster flashed to the buoy and swallowed it whole. The attached rope must have missed the severing teeth and lodged in the toothless, hinge section at the back of the jaw. The slack line tightened at my belt and I was wrenched forward and under the water again, dragged at shocking speed directly out to open sea. I tried to release my weight belt to which the line was attached, but my arms would not obey. We were moving like a torpedo now and had traveled to a depth of 30 or 40 feet. My left hand continued fumbling helplessly at the release catch. Normally I use my right hand for everything. Now my right hand was free and empty, yet I instinctively used my left hand to claw at the belt. Although I had no conscious realization of my injuries, there must have been some subconscious knowledge that four tendons had been cut, rendering the fingers on my right hand useless. My left arm was also in a bad way, slashed deeply beneath the triceps muscle.

Again, my hand slid down by my belly button to flick the quick-release—but there was no buckle. With the tow of the shark's great force pulling at the center of my body, my progress was erratic, a surging, swirling, spinning nightmare as I groped with my left hand to my right side, running fingers along the belt, groping for the quick release. The little air I had gulped down before being hauled back under was now exhausted. My mind became fuzzier every second. I realized that the belt must have slipped around my waist as the shark hauled me into the deep. I no longer had any air nor the strength to stretch my arm around my back in a final search for the buckle. Now, I was finished. I had done what I could.

Then a miracle occurred: right alongside my belt the rope snapped and I was free once more. Normally the rope would have taken more strain, but apparently when the shark had bitten me around the chest he had partly cut through the rope, leaving on a few strands intact. I kicked frantically up toward the light. They tell me that all I could scream when my head reached the surface was: "Shark! . . . Shark!" It was enough.

Now there were voices, familiar noises, then the boatful of friends I had been praying would come. I gave up trying to move and relied on them. I couldn't even offer my arms, they were so torn. They rolled me into the boat and I collapsed on the seat. They elevated my legs and raced for shore. In this new world of people, somebody kept saying, "Hang on, mate, it's over. Hang on." I think without that voice urging me on I would have died. On the way in, the patrol boat picked up a few more divers.

The men in the boat were horrified at the extent of my injuries. Bruce Farley was one fellow they had picked up on the way in; afterwards he told me he thought I was finished. Blood was pouring out of my wet suit and I was ghost white. My right hand and arm were so badly slashed that the bones lay bare in several places. My chest, back, left shoulder and side were deeply gashed. Great pieces of flesh had been torn aside, exposing the rib cage, lungs, and upper stomach. All my ribs on the left hand side were crushed, and the shoulder blade had a hole through it where a tooth had pierced the bone. My spleen was uncovered save for a membrane over the top, and the main artery of my heart was pulsing, exposed just along the side of the bite.

They raced the boat right up onto the rocky reef, not much caring if it destroyed the old wooden craft. Luckily the boat seats folded down into a 6-foot bed. I was only semi-conscious when men swarmed around from everywhere and dragged the boat right out of the water. Frank Alexander, who was president of the skin diver's association, had for the first time in fourteen years driven his car down onto the beach, tired as he was of walking up and down from the parking area on the cliff above with provisions for him, his wife, and three kids. The sand had packed just right, so the second the boat grounded onto the rocks, Frank drove his car onto the reef, bounding over huge potholes, right to the edge near the boat.

As they lifted me out of the boat the entire side of me opened up and loops of my intestines spilled out and hung down. They quickly rolled me up the other way. Malcolm Baker, who had studied first aid for his police examinations, tucked my intestines back with his fingers. They propped me up, stuck me in the back of Frank's Falcon, and he blasted back over the reef. Bruce Farley took off as soon as the boat hit the beach, running flat out. He asked the first person he saw where the nearest telephone was. The man was a policeman and knew where to go and what to do, and got an ambulance lined up immediately. In the back of Frank's

Falcon, Malcolm sat beside me and kept saying, "Keep trying, Rodney. Keep fighting. Just think of Kay and the baby. Come on, you've got to keep breathing!"

I could barely draw a breath. My left lung had collapsed and was in my throat or in the top of my chest. I kept trying to suck air into my right lung as hard as I could, while everything on my left side gurgled and sputtered. Malcolm kept repeating: "You've got to keep going."

I was barely cognizant. I could hear but couldn't understand much of what was happening. My only vivid sensation was swaying in the back of the car as we raced down the road at nearly 100 miles an hour. Someone put a hand on my chest and when he took it away I managed somehow to indicate it was better if he kept in there. I could not talk—being too busy trying to breath. I was sucking away with all my might and the hand on my chest stopped the wheezing and gurgling on my collapsed lung.

I heard the shouts: "Here's the ambulance! Stick a shirt out the window! Hang a towel out!" The Falcon screeched to a halt.

They transferred me to the ambulance on a stretcher and immediately gave me oxygen, which was probably the real lifesaver of the day. My fellow divers were only too pleased to hand me over to the experts. It told in their voices. It was a miracle I was still conscious. The doctor said that this was a big factor in my survival. Had I lost consciousness I probably would have died in the Falcon.

Police escorted us all the way to the hospital. From Aldinga to Adelaide is about 34 miles, and every stop light along the way was manned by policeman. We worked out later that from the time I was attacked till the time I reached the hospital was less than an hour.

The surgeons at Royal Adelaide Hospital were scrubbed and ready, the operating table felt warm and cozy, the huge silver light overhead grew dimmer . . . until late that night or early next morning I opened my eyes and saw Kay alongside my bed.

I said, "It hurts," and she was crying. The doctor walked over and said, "He'll make it now."

Today (1964), a year and a half later, my lungs work well, although my chest is still stiff. My right hand isn't a pretty sight but I can use it. My chest, back, abdomen, and shoulder are badly scarred.

God knows I didn't want to, but Kay realized from the start that I had to go skin diving again. A man's only half a man if fear ties him up. Five months after I recovered, I returned to the sea to leave my fears where I had found them.

Man-eaters!

Captain William E. Young

An account now seventy-five years old, "Man-eaters!" belongs to a bygone era when men like Captain Young were celebrated heroes whose books were introduced by counts and kings. Young claimed to have personally killed over 100,000 sharks. Much has changed in the ensuing decades, but not the irreducible brute element of the shark attack itself, nor the mixture of dread and curiosity triggered by the big predator, nor yet the odd crossings of fate that surround them.

Where the St. Mary's River empties into the Atlantic between Georgia and Florida there is a tremendous delta which has been building up for years. Shrimp fishing there is superb. Not a rock is to be found on the bottom, and, in the relatively shallow sea, millions of fish of all kinds common to the locality come to feed and breed. Sportsmen come there for the drum fish, but by and large the inhabitants of the section are professional fishermen.

Fernandina, a delightful town on the Florida side of the mouth, has long been noted for its shrimp fishing. Years ago pogie boats congregated there, but shrimp have proved more lucrative, and all that remains of the former days is a decidedly offensive smell from Pogietown when the wind is from the right quarter.

A muddy delta provides food desired by shrimp, the ants of the sea. Like their second cousins, the lobsters, shrimp eat anything found along the bottom. They come in droves, by the millions. And after them come small fish who feed on the shrimp. In turn, sharks are attracted by the shoals of fish.

A shrimp trawl is a tapering net affair with a wide mouth kept open by "legs" and spread lines, and measures perhaps 60 feet fore and aft when dragged along the bottom. The shrimp and other small fish are caught up by the net, and once within, the fish seldom find the way out again, although they try sticking their heads through the mesh. They are tempting to the first shark which happens to come along. He is greedy, and a great piece of the net comes away with each bite. The shark has found a free-lunch counter.

Sharks are the bane of the shrimp fishermen. Trailing the shrimp boats, they wreak havoc with equipment and schedules, and cause loss of temper, time and money. I have seen nets, probably worth seventy-five dollars, riddled by sharks and useless after a short two hours on the bottom. The only partial protection thus far devised by the fishermen is a slip-covering for the net made of cheesecloth which prevents the sharks from seeing and making for any protruding fish striving vainly to get through the meshes. Now and again a shark is captured in the net and killed with jubilation by the shrimp men.

They are even more eager to kill sharks now that a market is established for shark products. Until the time that we went to Fernandina, almost no commercial use had been discovered for sharks, except for the dried fins relished by the Oriental epicure. But if leather could be made from the hides, it meant that a carcass was worth saving. Even so, fishermen whose main business is catching shrimp are too busy at their own work to bother catching sharks, and those occasionally brought in by the shrimp fishermen were either caught in the shrimp net or on baited lines let over the stern as the boats trawled slowly along.

In the early morning, just at daybreak, the quiet surface is often broken by the sudden appearance of small Black-tip sharks leaping up into the air, twisting and turning, and falling back with a splash. Evidently the impact against their sides gives them a pleasurable feeling. The local fishermen can give no other reason for the display unless they do it because it "feels good." But the shrimp fishermen are not deceived; they know that larger beasts are waiting down below—waiting for the shrimp boats to put out for their morning catch.

Each boat seines, empties the catch on deck, and trawls again. The "junk" fish which clutter up the nets are dumped in one pile, shrimp are headed and thrown into the bins. When a large pile of heads and small fry has accumulated, a sailor grabs a scoop and shovels them over the side. Instantly all is confusion in the water.

Sharks which have been trailing the boats rush headlong toward the splash. So many reach the same spot at once and so great is their impetus that the spray often reaches the deck of the boat. Swirling and boiling, the sea is full of scrambling brutes. Within an amazingly short time not a vestige of the scraps is left.

When small sharks are active in this manner on the surface, there are invariably bigger sharks below the surface to pick up the heavier scraps. It is the so-called school sharks which travel on the top, feeding on the fish odds and ends. Down below are to be found the scavenger sharks, whose teeth enable them to be extremely catholic in their tastes. Both species cause great grief to the shrimp man, and he is anxious annihilate both—a rather difficult job for a shark will not take bait when it is thrown overboard; he is too foxy. The free fish tossed over will be instantly gobbled; the bait never. It is only by patient trolling with baited hooks that solitary sharks are lured to death, three or four being a fair catch for a day's work.

The shrimp fisherman is a hard worker. His season is from February to May with a short, less important fishing season at the end of the year. His day begins about two in the morning and ends around noon. His boat holds two, captain and deckhand. When sharks leave the nets alone, fishing is good.

Not long before I came to the Fernandina region, so they said, a fisherman had fallen overboard in the harbor from his boat. It was not very deep at that point, but sharks cruise even in the shallows of the delta for whatever luck offers. This time one happened to be near, evidently, for the man, a good swimmer, never came up.

"Shark," say the other fishermen laconically.

There isn't a man in the whole shrimp-fishing fleet who believes that sharks will not attack people. And even the negroes ashore are afraid to venture into deep water, although they know dark objects are fairly safe. When they see "dem ole gappin' jaws" they have no desire to become better acquainted and proceed to put considerable distance between themselves and the spot.

• • •

After the close of the summer at Nantucket, we had decided to move to a new station. Investigation led us to consider Fernandina as a likely shark fishing grounds. A man named Fagan, in charge of the phosphate bunkers of the Southern Railroad at Fernandina, had permission to use the docks, or part of them, for a skinning platform. He was a part-time shrimp fisherman and used to pick up sharks occasionally with his trolling lines. But the larger part of his hides came from the other shrimp boats for which he would pay a cent a pound. Fagan shipped his hides North for tanning and accordingly we knew the shark hunting was good down there.

For some time it had been the company's intention to send me there, mainly to take care of the hides collected by independent fishermen. The man formerly in charge of the station had enjoyed a profitable trade in liquor, but the trade in hides suffered. Fagan was put in charge of shore equipment, after demonstrating his ability to skin hides and pay attention to business.

I was not a landlubber for long; the old urge to go forth and do battle grew too strong to resist. Fagan assumed full charge of the station and I made ready a twenty-two-foot boat for under-running nets. One afternoon as I was preparing to set out on this new angle of the old game, a stranger put his head in at the door of the shed.

"Mister, do you know where I could find the boss?"

"Sure," I replied, "that's Fagan. But he's gone to town and won't be back before five o'clock. What's the trouble?"

"Nothing—I was curious about the shark fishing business, that's all. You see, I'm 'Pete, the Shark'—that's what they used to call me in the Navy. I'm bugs about sharks. All my life I've been interested in 'em and now I want to catch some if I can. How do you go about it, anyway?"

That was my introduction to Walter C. Johnston—who has proved himself to be the most ardent of shark fishermen. We went out to supper and talked nearly all night. Here I was about to launch myself as a shark hunter in strange waters off the Florida coast, and I could use a good hand. Without hesitation a deal was made. He had a job ready-made to fit him.

From then until Christmas, a matter of several months, we fished constantly. Johnston was a good man, conscientious and willing. But fishing there was none too good. Fagan had reduced his original offer of a cent and a half per pound to only a cent a pound. Besides, even the best fishing grounds peter out, making it necessary to keep on the move. So after several days of notable catches, our hauls were mediocre and finally not profitable.

On one of the great occasions of the early season, Johnston and I made a record catch. I had set the net adrift, floating with the tide instead of securing it with the anchors, so that it swept along the bottom at about three knots an hour. The rows of buoys on the surface were connected with short lines to the top line of the net. We didn't have to wait long. Suddenly the nearest buoy disappeared. We hauled in a big Tiger. Even before we had him secured, another buoy went out of sight. It was furious work. We pulled and tugged for four hours landing shark after shark, killing them and stowing the bodies in the cockpit until we scarcely had footage. Skates and rays were fairly common. When one came with the net, we cut it to permit the blood to escape and left it in the net. Better scent was not to be had, and it certainly brought plenty of sharks. In all, we caught 10,000 pound of shark that day.

When the thirty-sixth shark came aboard there was about 3 inches of freeboard left. And the net had to go ashore with us too. Fagan's shrimp boat finally arrived to take us in tow. We had such a load the water poured in through two small holes in the stern formerly used for securing a bumper. Not a stick of wood or a plug of any kind was available, and it was a long way in to the skinning platform. But I wasn't going to let that catch go to the bottom if I could help it, so I stuck my two thumbs in the holes and we got in safely.

In addition to skinning, Fagan was expert in rendering the liver oil of which every shark has such quantities. A 700-pound shark will contain a liver weighing well over a 120 pounds, and a great deal of it is clear yellow oil, high in medicinal content.

Fagan did his trying out with a three-barrel system that was very efficient. But, once as I was standing close by, the hose connection broke.

Instantly steam spurted out, hitting Fagan square in the face. His skin was fairly well cooked, and the live steam seared his eyes pretty badly. Quickly I reached over a tank of pure, cool shark oil and dipped up two handfuls. Calling out to him to drop his hands, I flung the stuff right in his face and eyes. He claims that it saved his eyes and I have no doubt that it did. For some hours he continued the treatment himself, until the pain subsided, and within a surprisingly few days his face returned to normal. Due to the action of the oil he had never been bothered with ill effects from the terrible scalding.

Sponge divers find shark oil unsurpassed for quieting the wind-tossed waves so that they may see down to the bottom. They spray it on the surface, where it spreads over a large area permitting excellent visibility.

Some time previous to this, investigators had been able to extract insulin from clams and other invertebrates of the sea. While I was at Fernandina, the Bureau of Fisheries sent a man down from Washington to buy up all the shark pancreas he could get, for further experimentation in obtaining insulin. If the trials had proved successful the shark would have been accorded some honor as an inexhaustible supply of this valuable aid in the treatment of diabetes.

By Christmas time the new director, who made casual visits to the station, decided that fishing had given out to an extent that warranted moving further South. We were to go after the first of the year. Fagan was dead set against it. He claimed that we couldn't shove off and leave him, quoting contracts and one thing and another. We told him we had to go just the same.

"All right," said Fagan, "let's see you go."

That was a challenge. On New Year's Eve about sundown, we set out, Fagan being up in town. We knew he would expect us to sail down the inside passage, for we had small boats. But instead of going down the river where we might have been stopped, we decided to take the outside passage. And so we set our course for Miami, 900 miles away.

It was something of a trip. But we were all tough and full of life. Going this way meant a rough voyage along the Florida coast instead of a cruise along the quiet waterways inside of the reef. It turned out a magnificent jaunt; the nights were beautiful; we had plenty to eat and not a care in the world.

While we were bucking the Gulf Stream some miles before coming abeam of Fort Lauderdale, the cooling system for the engine went bad, when the water pump gave out. We were threatened with all sorts of real trouble it we could not fix it, for the boat was heavily loaded with fishing gear. There were no materials on board for a repair job and for a while we were stumped. Then someone thought up a substitute dodge. We secured a fifty-gallon gasoline drum to the top of the deckhouse, cut its top off, and connected a hose from its bottom to the flange of the water jacket. Then all we had to do was pour water into the drum.

"Caibo," I said to the negro deckhand, "get up there with the bucket and line and fill that barrel."

"Okay boss," and he scrambled up with his gear.

The water ran down and cooled the engine just as well as if the pump had been fixed. Under way again we forgot our recent concern and began to sing as we lay on the net piled on the deck. But before long we were interrupted by a plaintive wail from the top of the deckhouse.

"Say boss," came an injured voice, "what good do it do fo'me to keep pourin' water into this barrel—it's all runnin'out the bottom fast as I put it in!"

When I could manage to speak, I said "Caibo, if you ever want to get to Fort Lauderdale, just keep on filling that barrel." Pretty soon we made port for repairs. Our substitute pump had done himself proud, but we have had many good laughs over Caibo and the water barrel.

Miami was our next stop. We were due for a great surprise. The monster shark of them all was on exhibition here, a Whale shark, thirteen and a half tons of shark meat all in one carcass! We stared for a long time, knowing that such a sight was seldom to be seen.

Captain Charles Thompson told me of the capture of the gargantuan creature: "We were anchored just below Knight's Key, about half a mile from the old Florida East Coast dock. Looking over there one morning about nine o'clock, I saw an unbelievably large shark within a few feet of the dock trestle. We immediately took to the launch and started after the fish, which was then near the trestle. I shouted to a man on the dock, asking if he had seen the shark. He replied that he had, but that it was no shark—and that he didn't know what it was. We got nearer and nearer until the boat was right over him and we could see his spotted back three or four feet below the surface. From this position I drove a harpoon into him near the gills. We called to some near-by fishermen to come help us, and with their assistance did everything we could think of to make him fast. Forty or fifty times during the day we shot at him with a rifle. At a distance of about 2 feet from his back we let fly with a shotgun loaded with No. 2 shot, which just bounced, leaving a little circular mark in his skin.

"Unruffled by our little attentions, this fish circled several times in from the trestle to perhaps half a mile inshore, coming back again and again, and about one o'clock in the afternoon when the tide was running out we thought he would get outside the bay. The boats were carried out by the tide, but the fish remained inside.

"I was surprised that he did not put up any fight and was so extremely sluggish. He seemed not to realize that anything in particular was happening to him, but kept circling around, moving his great tail, in a slow, regular way, drawing the small boats after him with the greatest ease. There were now several harpoons in him, and one line was fastened through his tail and another made fast to the dorsal fin.

"About half past five in the evening he made his last circle in from the trestle, and this time we headed him over toward a sand-bank by poking his head with a boat hook; he finally stranded on the sand-bank where he was made fast with lines around his body stretched to oars stuck deep in the sand. A piece was then cut from the top of his head and with a knife on the end of a pole, we tried to reach his brain and kill him. We were surprised to discover about 3 inches of gristle at this point in his head."

When the great catch was hauled out on the marine railway at Miami it broke the tackle, so massive was its bulk. Scientists from Washington hurried down to view the carcass, and were all agreed, after a careful examination, that this was a young specimen which had not yet attained its full growth. The skin, 4 inches thick, showed that the fish was a native of the deep sea, where the great pressure makes such a protection necessary. His comparatively small eyes were also characteristic of a deep-water fish. But, greatly to the disappointment of the landlubbers who flocked to see this curiosity, Captain Thompson's catch was not a ferocious man-eater. Within the stomach of this shark at the time of its capture they found a 200 pound jew-fish, part of a strange deep-sea octopus unknown to science, and 250 pounds of coral.

I stuck my head within the cavernous mouth to see for myself, and found the estimated 6,000 teeth—but they were all minute and useless for biting.

As it is impossible for a man to enter a whale's stomach, one of these Whale sharks probably deserves credit for being Jonah's submarine. While this shark was still in the water two men easily got within the great mouth as the head was partially raised by hook and chain.

Such a tremendous fish was a curiosity, but had no appeal for me. It would be poor sport indeed to participate in the capture of such a sluggish, defenseless thing. Besides, it is useless to commerce, for no tannery knows how to tan such a formidable hide.

Captain W. B. Caswell Sr., veteran Gulf fisherman of Panama City, Florida, told me once of a rather amusing incident which occurred near his home town some time ago.

"I had built a campfire in the palmetto," said Captain Casewell, "and was boiling a pot of coffee about two o'clock one morning. It had been a cold, raw night and my crew had made three long hauls over coral reefs. Just after midnight a big shark, striking at the gilled mackerel in the bunt, had torn our seine half in two. So we were out of business temporarily until it got light enough to see to mend our net.

"During the process of making coffee I heard the chug chug of a motor boat coming in the pass and recognized the exhaust of a boat belonging to a fisherman with whom I was well acquainted and who is now one our ablest Bar pilots. Coming abreast of my campfire the boat stopped and the captain sang out,

"That you, Captain Caswell?" On receiving an answer in the affirmative he said,

"How's coffee?"

"Sure," I answered. "Come ashore and join us."

In a moment or two we could hear the crew splashing in the shallows as they waded ashore and the Captain grumbling about something which was amiss. When they got near enough so that the light from our campfire shone on them, I looked up and inquired,

"What's wrong, Captain? Sharks eat your seine up too?"

"Seine heck!" he said, "look at me!" and then I saw what he meant— half his coat and the back of his trousers had been completely torn away.

"What happened?" I inquired.

"Well," he grumbled, "I was holding the lead line down in a swash below the Bell Shoals and we caught a seine full of sharks along with the mackerel, and one took a nip at me. Them slickers cost me six dollars and them dungarees cost one dollar and ninety cents—best duck brand—and that flannel underwear cost me three dollars a suit and I had a big bandanna handkerchief in my hip pocket and he got that too. Enough to make a man swear." Even the coffee failed to cheer him up, and he went back to the boat grumbling about having to buy a new outfit the next day. Such is the life of a fisherman.

At Key West we got a scow and took it up to Big Pine Key to be used as a temporary skinning platform until a shore station could be completed. We had four boats and a lot of gear on hand, so we began fishing right away. It proved good, and we used to bring in great numbers of Nurse sharks. At that time the leather company did not know how to tan this skin, and we were ordered not to ship such hides North. Now, however, they will accept all such sharks caught, for a particularly fine brand of leather can be made from the hide.

Pete the Shark, and I again teamed up together against the many species of sharks to be captured in the Gulf Stream. Every day our nets bulged with fish, and we brought in tons to the skinning platform. I was always curious to discover what it was that each shark had been eating, and I found that their diet was most varied: Junk fish, crabs and lobsters, turtles, many horseshoe crabs, sea urchins, other sharks, tin cans, bottles, and, in short, almost anything afloat or on the bottom. In the stomach of one I remember finding eight horseshoe crabs as big as washbasins and with hooks and spines, in the process of digestion. Shark digestive enzymes are powerful enough to soften their shells in a short time. Once some of his digestive fluid spilled on my foot, and soon the skin came off as if I had been badly burned.

In my travels in mid-Pacific and up and down the Atlantic Coast I have met many people who stoutly claimed that sharks were maligned and did not attack human beings. But I have never found any natives or seafaring men who were as sure of it as most of these wiseacres from ashore. I have never heard anyone familiar with sharks and their habits state that they believe them harmless. To the contrary, yarns of tiger-like ferocity are a stock in trade with fishermen and sailors of all lands. The black men or the brown-skinned men have little fear of scavenger sharks, principally because they realize that in waters free from blood or fresh-meat scent, a shark will hesitate to take a dark object. In the Barbados I learned the natives before entering even shallow water are most particular to smear their hands and feet with tar so that the whiter skin will not flash against the dark blue water. They know that it is always the hand or foot which is first attacked. The diving boys that risk running afoul of sharks when going after tossed coins do not depend on the knives of fable to overcome armor-plated fish. They make for their canoes as fast as they can if danger threatens. And the white-skinned Australian has a healthy dread of going swimming even in the surf, where many of the biggest so-called man-eaters have been netted.

Johnston and I had fished well one morning. And, as usual, we were completing the day's work by skinning off the hides and preparing them for shipment. Since it is my habit to investigate the contents of the shark belly, I tackled the stomach of a twelve-foot Brown shark with my knife. I noticed an odd protuberance on the stomach wall, and slit the lining a bit. The round end of a bone came out. I grasped it with one hand and cut further, finding some flesh attached to the bone. And in withdrawing the entire object I was horrified to find it a recently swallowed arm with the hand intact—a human arm and right hand. The crew crowded around and for a while there was no thought of work to be done. The arm was in a good state of preservation, indicating that it had been in the shark only a few hours. The palm of the hand and finger-tips were wrinkled as if from long contact with the water, and it was the hand of a man not used to manual toil. There were no rings or tattoo marks to be seen.

Acting on the suggestion that perhaps the stomach contained identifying material, I sought further and brought to view six pieces of human flesh and a square of blue cloth from a man's coat. Evidently the shark had dined well. Since no other bones were discovered, we agreed that sharks had attacked the body in a group and, after preliminary bites, had lunged and snapped at the flesh, each gulping as much as possible. It would have been comparatively simple for the shark we caught to swallow the arm once it was torn from its socket; and it went down entire, hand first, followed by the pieces of flesh salvaged from the horrid feast.

We discussed what we should do with it. Finally Johnston took his knife, severed the hand at the wrist, and placed the relic in preservative in a jar. We sent it to the coroner.

The rest went overboard.

The further developments in this story I quote from the N.Y. *News*.

. . . On the morning of January 13, 1923, Edwin F. Atkins, Jr., and his family, accompanied by a nurse and a governess, boarded a twin-motored seaplane *Columbus*, operated by Aeromarine Airways, Inc., to fly to Havana, forty miles away. Atkins had frequently made use of the airplane, which maintained a regular daily schedule between Key West and Havana, with a record of no mishaps.

The two children, after take-off, went to sleep in the aft cabin. The day was calm but the sea was choppy. All went well for while. The Atkins entourage had been joined by Otto Abrahams, a New York banker and broker, as a fellow passenger. The plane's crew consisted of a pilot and a mechanic.

Twenty miles from Havana, the starboard motor began to miss, and C. W. Miller, the pilot became anxious. He sought to remedy the defect, but at length determined that he could not go farther. The plane had been proceeding at 65 miles per hour, and at 200-foot altitude. Miller looked about for a spot to alight in the Gulf Stream. He found the water very rough, but when he espied a ferryboat below he determined to come down at once.

The *Columbus* came down at 45 miles an hour. One of the surging waves—15–20 feet in height—struck the pontoons and the plane was catapulted into the air. Before Miller could right the ship it came down nose first into a swell, and another wave spun the airship completely around.

The aft cabin was submerged almost immediately, and the terrific impact tossed the occupants to all corners of the larger forward cabin. The two children were never seen again and it was probable they were killed by the first shock.

When Atkins, dazed, realized the condition of the aft cabin, he was restrained with difficulty by Abrahams and the mechanic, Harold Thompson, from plunging into it. Despite restraint, Atkins and the governess, Grace McDonald, climbed out of the cabin and out on the wings. There they clung.

Meanwhile, the ferryboat H. M. *Flagler,* which plied daily between Key West and Havana, was bending all efforts to reach the stricken airliner. The *Flagler,* under Capt. John Albury, launched a lifeboat with great difficulty, but time and again it was swept away from the plane wreckage but the surging seas.

A wave crashed over the wings of the plane and swept Miss McDonald from her perch. Then another wave, a huge one struck the wreck and Atkins was swept into the sea.

Passengers lined the ferryboat's rails to watch the proceedings with agonized eyes. At length the two women were taken aboard the lifeboat and the others clambered aboard, too.

Meanwhile, the sister air liner of the *Columbus,* the *Ponce de Leon,* hovered overhead. But it was powerless to aid. It was more than an hour before all in the lifeboat were safely aboard the ferry.

Mrs. Atkins, the nurse, Julia Haverty, Abrahams, the pilot,

Miller, and the mechanic were saved. Atkins, his two boys, Edwin and David, and the governess, Grace McDonald, perished.

Next day Atkins's brother, Robert, chartered a ferry steamer at Havana to search for the bodies of the four who were lost. He offered a reward of $4,000 for their recovery.

On the day following, at Big Pine Key, Florida, 40 miles north of Key West, Capt. W. E. Young, Walter C. Johnston, and their men were engaged in their regular business—netting sharks for their leather and teeth. They pulled in a Brown shark measuring nearly 12 feet in length. Capt. Young told of the discovery:

"I proceeded to rip him open and was amazed to find a human arm and hand in the Brown shark. I was particularly surprised because the Brown shark is not usually regarded as a vicious killer. I immediately got my camera and made several pictures.

"I also found pieces of human flesh in this same shark and a piece of blue serge cloth about 12 inches by 18, that appeared to have been part of a coat.

"The arm to the elbow was not mangled, but from there up to where it ended—at the shoulder joint—all the flesh had been torn away. The six pieces of flesh in the Brown shark were not enough to account for the whole part torn away, so I concluded that two or maybe three sharks had come upon the man's body, floating arms downward—a woman floats all doubled up, you know—and had joined in tugging at it.

"I began to make inquiries about anybody being lost lately, and then I heard about the Atkins' disaster. I notified the coroner at Key West and he came up to Big Pine Key.

"In the meantime, Johnston had cut off the hand from the arm and preserved it in a glass jar of alcohol.

"The coroner examined all the stuff we found and took it along with him. I understood from some of Atkins' friends, both at Key West and in Havana, that he was wearing a blue serge coat, and when I described the hand to them they agreed it was undoubtedly his.

"But none of them cared to look at the hand."

The day following the discovery of the hand, Johnston and I went with the cloth fragment to the aviation field at Key West. There we interviewed a friend of Atkins, who sadly identified the piece as being from Atkins's coat, which he had worn when goodbye was said. Upon such identification the reward for the recovery of the body was withdrawn. Sharks had infested that portion of the sea, our catch coming up North with the Gulf Stream after his feed.

But the strange paths of coincidence were not content to let the gruesome matter rest here. I was going down to Porto Rico on a steamer two years afterward and fell into conversation with a man and his wife sitting at my table. I showed my shark teeth pictures to them, and the man turned away with a gasp from the photograph I always carried in answer to the inevitable question "Will sharks eat human beings?" I pressed him for the reason he felt repugnance.

"Why," he said, "the widow of this poor fellow is marrying my best friend!"

The following year, when journeying from St. Thomas to Trinidad, I was showing the pictures again in the smoking-room after dinner, another Boston man was similarly shocked at the photograph. In this case the man had been a boyhood chum of the unfortunate planter, and was greatly grieved.

Six months later while I was lecturing on sharks in Deerfield, Massachusetts, a total stranger from Boston, Dr. Harry A. Barnes, told me that a relative of his wife had met a man down in the West Indies who had showed him a photograph of a hand found within a shark stomach—the hand taken from the body of a close friend of his. I let him tell his story, then exhibited the identical photographs to his astonished gaze. I was growing squeamish about showing the photograph, and felt that another meeting with a friend of Atkins should result in saying no more about the incident. The pictorial proof was bringing too much direct, horrible evidence of the planter's death to former friends.

In 1930 I was conferring in Cuba with government officials about the establishment of a unique aquarium, and in offering substantiation on past experience, I again showed the photograph. The reaction was immediate, for many of them had known the man.

"Señor Atkins! *Tiburon, muy grande!*" Yes, a big shark. The picture had been viewed once again by past friends, and I was determined to use it no more. But other people would not let the matter rest. Wherever I have gone the same question is raised invariably: "Do sharks eat human beings?" I have satisfied myself on this point, and the photograph of Johnston holding the arm is enough. . . . It speaks more authoritatively than pages of hearsay and quotations. It is fearful, and to many, gruesome indeed. But it may induce people to take caution when they plan to bathe in waters known to contain sharks. I know it has done so in the past.

When in Australian waters some time later I met with even more savage man-eaters than those which cruised the warm Florida seas, but there it was entirely superfluous to exhibit any such picture. The tale it tells is only too well known there.

The Final Parade

The story of the wreck of the English paddle frigate Birkenhead off South Africa is notorious in the annals of shark attacks. While we can only speculate how many of the 455 who died were taken by sharks, this account suggests the number was considerable. Note the cool, deliberate actions of those doomed in this historic sea epic, as though order and dignity were prized even above life itself.

At 2:00 A.M. on February 26, 1852, the paddle frigate *Birkenhead,* carrying 490 soldiers of the British Army, with twenty-five of their wives and thirty-one children, together with a crew of 134, struck a reef about 1.6 kilometers (1 mile) off Danger Point near the southern tip of Africa.

In the first few minutes following the collision, confusion reigned. Seamen, soldiers, and passengers struggled onto the deck to escape water rapidly filling the ship as she settled at the bow.

On deck the officers moved quickly to establish calm, ordering the men to fall on the poop. Lieutenant Colonel Alexander Seton, the senior army commander aboard, called his officers together and calmly requested them to make sure that any orders given by the ship's captain were instantly obeyed.

Captain Salmond ordered the women and children in a lifeboat, detailing an ensign and a sergeant to forcibly separate women who clung desperately to their men. A second lifeboat with thirty men aboard was lowered into the swell. For the 600 remaining aboard the dangerously listing ship there were no lifeboats. Many trapped below decks had already drowned. Many more had been killed by falling wreckage or swept overboard. From the water came the terrified screams as floundering swimmers were dragged down by packs of sharks that cruised around the doomed ships. The 200 survivors still able to stand supporting those who were not, stood fast on the poop deck.

Salmond climbed a few meters up the mizzen rigging and shouted to the men: "Save yourselves all those who can swim jump overboard and make for the boats. That is your only hope of salvation." Lieutenant Colonel Seton was appalled. The lifeboats were already dangerously full. If 200 soldiers tried to board them, the boats would be lost.

Seton raised his hand above his head and shouted: "You will swamp the cutter containing the women and children. I implore you not to do this thing, I ask you all to remain where you are." Some survivors later said that three men went over the rail, but of the rest of the 200, not a man moved. They stood rigidly to attention. Moments after Seton's command, the *Birkenhead* broke its back, the bow slid beneath the water and the stern reared up. A surviving officer wrote later: "Every man did as he was directed and there was not a cry or murmur among them until the vessel made her final plunge. . . . [The officers] had received their orders and had carried them out as if the men were embarking instead of going to the bottom of the sea. There was only one difference—I never saw any embarkation conducted with so little noise or confusion."

The *Birkenhead* went down just thirty minutes after striking the rocks. Within a short time all but a handful of those that had survived the sinking were dead. On the surface of the water, stained crimson with blood, floated the barely recognizable remains of those torn apart by sharks.

Lieutenant Frank Girardot later described what happened in a letter to his father: "I remained on the wreck until she went down. The suction took me down some way and a man got hold of my leg, but I managed to kick him off and came up and struck for some pieces of wood. . . . I was in the water about five hours . . . the surf ran so high that a great many were lost trying to land. Nearly all those that took to the water without their clothes on were taken by the sharks; hundreds of them were all around us and I saw men taken quite close to me, but as I was dressed . . . they preferred the others."

More than sixty men made the 1.6-kilometer (1-mile) swim to shore and safety—though most of the men aboard the *Birkenhead* could not swim, including Alexander Seton who drowned. Captain Salmond was thrown overboard and died in the water when struck by a piece of falling wreckage. The wreck claimed 455 lives, but the proportion claimed by the ship, the sea, and the sharks is one of the mysteries of that dreadful night. One of the survivors, Captain Wright, said later that, but for the discipline of the men, the loss of life would have been still higher.

DEATH IN NEW JERSEY

In 1916, as America was being pulled into the maelstrom of World War I, an extraordinary series of shark attacks left three men and one boy dead, with a second boy badly injured, all in the space of just twelve days. The sleepy towns on the New Jersey coast, just south of New York, were thrust into the national press, and the "shark menace" even claimed the attention of President Woodrow Wilson and his cabinet.

T he panic came slowly. On July 1, 1916, a twenty-five-year-old Philadelphia fine arts graduate, Charles E. Vansant, was swimming 15 meters (16 yards) from the shore at Beach Haven, New Jersey, in the United States, when people on the beach saw a black fin slicing toward him and shouted at him to get out. Vansant splashed madly for the beach. As the shark closed on him, he screamed for help, then went under. An Olympic swimmer on the beach dashed into the water and pulled the badly mauled Vansant ashore. He died in the hospital the following night.

The tragedy stirred no great unease along the Jersey shore, and still less in Manhattan, where the editors of the *New York Times* placed a two-paragraph report of the attack on page 18. It was one of the minor tragedies of summer, like a swimmer hit by lightning.

Five days later the level of anxiety on the Jersey shore made a quantum leap upwards. On July 6, Charles Bruder, a bellboy at a Spring Lake, New Jersey hotel, was attacked while swimming beyond the lifelines. A woman on shore cried that she saw a red canoe beneath the waves, but the "canoe" was pumping from Bruder's severed legs. He died on the beach. Lifeguards and old Spring Lake residents told a *New York Times* reporter that this was the only shark attack at the resort that they could remember. The *Times* editors placed the story with details of women "fainting" and "panicking" on page one. Spring Lake hotel staff raised $1,000 to send to Bruder's mother in Switzerland.

Although Bruder's death kept swimmers close to shore at Spring Lake the next day, even this elementary precaution extended no more than a few kilometers away. But the businessmen of local resort towns, naturally assuming that news of shark attacks would not help to attract summer holidaymakers, wanted reassuring official action—and Spring Lake mayor, Oliver H. Brown, immediately established a motor boat patrol. The boats dragged bleeding quarters of lamb as bait while marksmen with rifles stood ready to shoot should a fin materialize. None did. The Mayor also ordered the beach bathing area enclosed in a sharkproof wire net, a precaution also taken by the nearby resort of Asbury Park.

Fishermen and surfers ridiculed these precautions, pointing out that no shark had ever been sighted off Asbury Park. Academic experts were also reassuring: Dr. A. T. Nichols, the American Museum of Natural History's shark expert, said that there was "very little chance" of a shark ever attacking anyone. The museum's director, Dr. Frederick A. Lucas, said there was more chance of being struck by lightning than being attacked by a shark, and in any case, sharks' jaws were not powerful enough to bite through a human legbone. The captain of a trans-Atlantic liner said he was "astounded" to learn of a man-eating shark off the New Jersey coast; this was the first time he had heard of one north of the Bahamas. A report in the *New York Times* of July 11 said "Tiger sharks will hold but little terror for bathers in the waters hereabouts within the next few days" because of the netting at Asbury Park.

It was a classic piece of predictive journalism: within twenty-four hours sharks were part of every conversation on the Jersey shore.

July 12 brought tropical heat and humidity to Matawan, New Jersey, a small town 17 kilometers (11 miles) west of the Atlantic shore, linked to the ocean by a meandering tidal creek. At 2:00 P.M. Lester Stilwell, a twelve-year-old boy employed at the town's sawmill, was given the afternoon off because of the stifling heat. With four friends, he headed for the Wyckoff Dock, a dilapidated old steamboat pier on Matawan Creek which was the town's most popular swimming hole—throughout the summer naked boys would liberate themselves from heat and boredom by playing on the exposed dock pilings.

Shortly before Lester and his friends headed for the creek, Captain Thomas Cottrell, a retired sailor was walking across a new Matawan

Creek bridge about 750 meters (833 yards) downstream from the swimming hole. He saw beneath the sparkling creek surface a huge black shadow moving quickly upstream with the incoming tide. Cottrell did not step to tell himself that no shark could be that far upstream, he ran for a telephone and called the town's barber, John Mulsonn, who was also the chief of police. Then he ran to Main Street telling groups of boys headed for the creek, merchants and their customers: "There's a shark in the creek!" People thought he was crazy: a shark? in a creek 10 meters (11 yards) across at its widest? Clam diggers worked the shallows at low tide: Poor old Tom's eyes must have been playing tricks on him. As Chief Mulsonn stropped his razor he reflected that people tell policemen some crazy stories.

Lester Stilwell, who suffered from "fits," was a strong swimmer. He was floating further away from the pier than his friends when they saw him suddenly disappear, re-emerge, scream, then disappear in a flurry. His friends sprinted into Matawan shouting that Lester had a fit in the creek and had disappeared in the water.

Stanley Fisher, a likeable, popular man of twenty-four, who had just started a dry-cleaning business, was one of the many who heard the boys' shouts. Stanley, a 95-kilogram (210-pound) blonde giant, had recently been mocked by his friends for accepting a $10,000 life insurance policy instead of cash in payment for a suit. He was nuts, they said. You? Life insurance? At twenty-four? You must be joking. The good-natured Stanley just smiled quietly.

As Fisher ran for the creek, he passed a woman acquaintance, a Matawan teacher, who shouted: "Remember what Captain Cottrell said. It may have been a shark." Fisher barely paused. "A shark here?" he said. "I don't care—I'm going after that boy."

Men, women, and children were streaming from the town to the pier, among them Lester Stilwell's parents. As Fisher yanked on his bathing trunks and plunged into the creek about 200 people lined the banks while men in rowing boats poled for Stilwell's body.

The urgency of the action, the need for something—anything—in the face of tragedy must have driven Stanley Fisher, for in his rational mind surely knew that if Lester was still beneath the creek he must have drowned, or worse. But the urgency of the moment was very powerful: several other men were also in the creek, making repeated dives, clawing along the mud for the boy's body. After several midstream dives, Fisher surfaced and shouted to the watchers on the bank: "I've got it." He had a grip on Lester's body and struck out for the nearer shore, opposite the pier, followed by two men in a motorboat. He stood up in waist-deep water near the bank, then staggered, cried out, and dropped into a crouch. From the motorboat, Detective Arthur Van Buskirk saw Fisher with both hands clamped around his right leg—the outside of his thigh, from hip to knee, was missing. Van Buskirk pulled him into the boat. On the dock men improvised a stretcher from planks and carried him, still conscious, 250 meters (273 yards) to the Matawan railroad. He was placed aboard the 5:06 train from Long Branch. At 7:45, as he was being wheeled into the operating theater of the Monmouth Memorial Hospital, he died. The townspeople—frightened and angered by the monster who had killed a boy just on the verge of leaving childhood, and one of Matawan's most personable young men, in one unbelievable afternoon of horror—collected dynamite and set underwater charges by the pier. They had two hopes: the blasts might kill the shark and they might force Stilwell's body to the surface.

Just as the charges were ready for blasting, a motorboat roared upstream to the pier with another shark victim. Joseph Dunn, a fourteen-year-old from upper Manhattan, had been swimming with several other boys off a dock 800 meters (867 yards) downstream from the Wyckoff pier when someone ran up with a warning: "There's been two shark attacks upstream—get out of the water!" The boys struck out quickly for the dock. Joseph, the last out, was on the ladder when the shark seized his right leg. "I felt my leg going down the shark's throat—thought it would swallow me," he said. At first Dunn would not give his name because he was afraid his mother would worry about him. Seriously injured, with much of the flesh below the knee stripped from his leg, he was rushed to St. Peter's Hospital in New Brunswick.

While a surgeon cleaned and stitched Joseph's severed tendons and lacerated leg muscles, Matawan Creek boiled and spurted geysers as if a primal force had been let loose between its tranquil banks. As indeed it had. In the grip of anger fuelled by fear, the men of Matawan purchased all the town's dynamite in a few hours. Before the sun set the town was also out of ammunition: hundreds of men lined the creek banks armed with shotguns. Those without guns brought pitchforks, knives, boat-hooks, antique harpoons ripped from living-room walls—even hammers. A small army of newspaper reporters and photographers descended on the creek, while newsreel cameramen filmed the vengeful fury and some-times added to it—especially large charges pushed white geysers high above the creek for the benefit of the newsreels. Shark sightings, and sightings of shadows, were as common as the claims in the low-tide ooze, especially by lanternlight. With the incoming tide, sightings abounded; with the outgoing tide, escaping sharks abounded. A chicken-wire net was strung across the creek just above Wyckoff Dock, and a strong fish-net across the bridge where Captain Cottrell sighted the black shadow. But two days after the tragedy the orgy of vengeance had yielded noth-ing, and Lester Stilwell's body had still not been recovered.

While the men who sought relief in action shot and dynamited the creek, others who sought the relief of understanding tried to answer the questions: what sort of shark was it, and why these unprecedented attacks at this time?

Dr. A. T. Nichols, at the American Museum of Natural History, believed a single shark was responsible for all the attacks. He thought it was a Great White or tiger shark which had got out of the Gulf Stream, could no longer find the green turtles which were its staple diet, and had developed a taste for human flesh after the attack on Charles Vansant.

Some local fishermen blamed the Germans: World War I had reduced the number of passenger ships entering New York Harbor which tossed refuse overboard, so the sharks were naturally looking for an alter-native source of food.

Although the *New York Times* loftily opined from the safety of its office on West 43rd Street in Manhattan that "sharks have a much better right to kill us than we have to kill them," dozens of sharks were being hooked, shot and dynamited. On April 14, funeral services for Lester

Stilwell, whose body had not been recovered, and Stanley Fisher were conducted in Matawan. The same day, a Manhattan taxidermist, who had caught a 2.4-meter (5-foot) shark off New Jersey, exhibited two bones found in its stomach—one of them identified by physicians as a boy's shinbone.

Joseph Dunn survived. Fifty-nine days after the attack, he left St. Peter's Hospital. His leg would always bear the purple scars, but he was able to walk away.

Lester Stilwell's body was eventually found 100 meters (110 yards) upstream from Wyckoff Dock three months after the attack; it was marked by seven bites. On the same day, President Woodrow Wilson's cabinet met in Washington and devoted much of the agenda to the shark menace. The Treasury Secretary promised to instruct the Coast Guard to "use every means for driving the sharks away or killing them," although he acknowledged that the Coast Guard "really couldn't do too much about man-eating sharks anyway."

The Director of the Museum of Natural History, Dr. Lucas, offered newspaper reporters the insight that the reason for the attacks was that "1916 is a shark year, just as we have butterfly years and army-worm years."

Three days after Lester Stilwell's' body was found, the mayors of ten New Jersey coastal resorts issued a statement protesting the news reports which "cause the public to believe the New Jersey seacoast is infested with sharks, whereas there are no more than any other summer."

The resort business, the mayors said, had been "hurt without cause" by the news focus on sharks. Their towns lost an estimated $1 million in holiday cancellations.

SURFING WITH THE GREAT WHITE SHARK

Kenny Doudt

The craggy, mist-shrouded Oregon coastline is at once enchanting for its wild gray seascape, and foreboding for the same reason. The surfers who ply these waters hope for good swells and expect cold water and foggy days. However, the presence of a Great White shark in their lineup, so close to shore, was never expected—and Kenny Doudt was not expected to survive his grim encounter with the predator.

I paddled out alone through the ice-cold beach break, paddling hard not only to keep my blood circulating but to get back out to the lineup. As I paddled toward the four others, I relived the ride I had just taken. Stoked by the feeling, I couldn't wait to catch another one.

I could see Josh and Al paddling out in the rip next to the north side of Haystack. Steve and Jack were also visible, sitting on their boards, shivering while they waited for the next good set. We all were totally unaware that one of the nature's great predators had just circled the outside rim of the rock and had glided beneath them as it moved swiftly, noiselessly, in a direction parallel to the shore.

It is impossible to know why the creature ignored the four surfers as it passed beneath them. I guess, since I was paddling hard to make it through the already crashing wave, the shark was attracted to the outline of my body as the sun shone through the water. Most likely my wet suit-covered legs and my black-gloved hands moving rhythmically through the water made me resemble a seal lion, a Great White's favorite meal.

There was no warning. Floating on his board about fifty feet away, Steve stared in total disbelief as a mass of light gray rose out of the water, back arching, mouth agape, gill slits flapping, pectoral fins horizontal and rows of razor-sharp teeth exposed. Paralyzed with terror, he watched helplessly as the shark instantly grabbed me and submerged me under the surface.

Oddly, I was not at first fully aware of the danger. I heard a muffled roar as the shark's massive jaws clamped across my back, pressing the board into my chest. Puzzled at what was happening, but feeling no pain, I thought I was being attacked by a sea lion. The shark pulled me two feet under water, but couldn't hold me under due to the buoyancy of the surfboard. The Great White's jaw was wide enough to cover an area from my armpit to the middle of my buttocks in a half-pie shape a mere half inch away from my spine.

Not yet fully aware of what was happening, I felt tremendous pressure on my chest and heard ribs snapping and the crunching of the underside of my board as the shark turned out to sea. I felt totally helpless, as my entire body was lifted high above the water, then slammed back down beneath the surface as the shark attempted to rip and tear my body apart, its usual method of killing and eating its prey. However, the buoyancy of the board kept it from diving deep. If the shark has been able to keep me under the water, it probably would have drowned me.

Steven and Jack were scared out of their minds. They knew exactly what was happening. I still thought I was an angry sea lion, many of which were annoyed by surfers around Haystack Rock chasing away the fish they generally fed on.

Feeling no pain and being totally helpless, I could not determine what was happening until the shark turned on its right side and allowed me a full view of his its long, massive, silver-gray body and huge dorsal and pectoral fins. Only then did I know what had me! Terror-stricken, I watched its five-foot-long pectoral fin break the surface, followed by the waving of its tail fin some 15 feet behind. I could not take my eyes off of it as it surged back and forth, beating the water into a froth.

It finally dawned on me that I was in the process of being eaten by a gigantic shark, exactly as I had seen in the movie *Jaws!*

The shark continued to violently shake me back and forth as a dog would with a bone or rag doll. I could hear Steven screaming and warning at Jack. Both were too paralyzed with fear to do more than watch their friend being devoured by a shark. When my eyes met Steve's he was paddling for shore. He knew there was nothing he could do and so did I.

"Help me! Help me! Please, help!"

Defenseless, beyond anyone's help, I continued to struggle impotently, trying to twist loose, hitting the shark on its head. I was taken back under, fully expecting to see the lower half of may body ripped off and float away.

For the third time the shark lifted me high out of the water, shaking me unmercifully as I pounded its head with my fist. I could see its silver tail thrashing the water, my body snapping so hard, I was sure this was it. It seemed my life was at an end. The mauling began to subside and I made eye contact with Jack, still sitting on his board, his mouth agape and his eyes wide with horror.

When he heard me scream, the spell was broken and he began to paddle away, at the same time shouting a warning to Josh and Al who had paddled out in the rip still unaware of the attack.

"Go back! Get out of the water! Kenny is being attacked by a huge shark!" They paused. "I'm not kidding you. A shark's got him."

By then Steve was paddling like crazy for shore, not realizing he was on a collision course with the shark and me. Luckily, Steve looked up in time to change his direction. Now he was even more terrified, expecting at any moment to find himself under attack.

Josh and Al heard the yelling but continued to paddle out toward the surf, not yet understanding the danger they were in. Finally, they both saw what was happening.

"Jesus," mumbled Josh at last seeing the shark. He yanked his board around and paddled to the beach, thinking that the shark might block his way.

"Holy shit! Look, Al! Do you see that? Let's get the hell outta here," shouted Josh. Al, having finally noticed, paddled his kneeboard with all his might, adrenalin feeding his muscles. Neither expected to make it to shore without a confrontation with the shark. The beach seemed to take forever to reach.

There was no way I could blame any of them for leaving me. There was absolutely nothing, under the circumstances any of them could have done for me. I had a terrible feeling of abandonment, being left alone in the ocean, locked in the jaws of a shark. All I could do was to beat my fists and scream, praying in my mind, watching my life pass before me, sure I was dead meat. Worst of all was the sadness I felt, knowing I would never again see my sons.

Later I estimated the shark held me in its jaws for about twenty seconds. It seemed closer to an hour, the longest short period of my life. Then suddenly the pressure was released and I was floating on the surface of the ocean about 20 feet from my surfboard. My surf leash, made out of half-inch bungee cord, had snapped like a piece of thread. I could not believe my luck. Still terrified, I looked all around for the shark. It had disappeared below the surface. I fully expected it to hit me again. A circle of blood-red water surrounded me as I treaded water about 100 yards from the beach.

The fear of another attack pumped a charge of adrenalin into my bloodstream, giving me the strength to swim the twenty feet to my board and pull myself on top of it. Blood poured from my wounds, enlarging the circle of blood around me. I was surprised to find my legs and arms still attached and that I was not paralyzed.

Drawing strength from an unknown source, I paddled like a madman, legs bent at the knees, feet as high as I could hold them. My primary fear what that a second attack would sever them from my body. I gasped for air between sobs of fear, expecting at any second to feel the shark's jaws clamp down on my body and pull me back to sea to die alone.

I could hear myself pleading, as I kept moving my arms, "Let me see my sons again. Please God, let me see them again."

Although I felt no pain, I knew I had been badly hurt. Blood ran down my arms and over my hands as I paddled. I could hear myself breathing through the rip in my back, a mixture of air and blood gurgling in and out with each breath. It sounded like the noise made when you squeeze a nearly empty ketchup bottle. I was afraid to touch my back or try to look at it, knowing if I saw my own blood gushing out, I would pass out and never make it back to shore.

A crashing sound behind me sent a wave of terror through my body. I expected to feel the shark's teeth sink into my legs, but instead was

relieved when I looked over my right shoulder and it was a wave breaking, its force lifting the rear of my board and pushing me toward the
beach. The foam from the crashing wave was a deep red. I had only
enough strength to grab the rails with my hands and hold on tight with
all my might, leaving my deliverance to the power of the ocean.

My own strength finally deserted me. My head drooped to the
board and my arms dragged limply alongside. My only hope was that I
had gotten into water too shallow for the shark to follow.

Josh, Jack, and Al, standing at the water's edge, stared in disbelief as
the dwindling wave pushed me in their direction. None had given me the
slightest chance of surviving the brutal attack by the biggest shark any of
them had ever seen. The foam on either side of me was red and was a fading trail out to sea.

Steve, who had reached the beach first, had paused only long enough
to unstrap his surf leash, then race across the sand to phone for help, knowing he had to do all he could to save my life after what he had just seen.

I felt the sand rub against my finger tips as the wave subsided in less
than knee deep water. I was too weak to lift my head or to move even my
fingers. Blood bubbled from ribs and wounds all along my back. The
sound of air rushing in and out with each breath scared me worse than
anything else. Oddly, I had not lost consciousness, nor felt much pain. All
I felt was relief that I had made it to shore.

Now, out of the monster's reach, I was ready to die.

Josh, Jack, and Al began to draw the attention of the people on the
cliff above, especially surfers just about to head for the ocean.

Two whose attention were immediately caught were Tom and
Mike, who were just pulling on their wet suits at Mike's girlfriend's house
above Haystack Rock.

Tom pointed at the growing crowd below. "Isn't that a surfer in
trouble just inside the white water? He must be badly hurt. I can see
blood in the water around him."

"Jesus. I wonder who it is?" Asked Mike.

"Gotta be someone we know," Tom answered.

"Let's get down there and see if we can help."

The two rushed from the house, jumping into Mike's care, slamming the doors shut as they roared off down to the beach.

Al, Jack, and Josh, without any thought that they might be in danger if the shark followed me into the shallow water, rushed to my aid. The water around me was deep red. No one thought I could possibly be alive after losing the amount of blood which was pouring out of numerous wounds across my back. The flow was only partially stemmed by the tattered remnants of my wet suit. When they got to me, they could see white rib ends protruding through torn flesh as they turned me on my side. What appeared to be gallons of blood poured from inside of my wet suit, turning the water an even darker red.

"Jesus," exclaimed Al. "We gotta get him out of the water before the shark gets him again!"

They would actually see exposed organs pulsating beneath broken ribs. My heart, with each contraction, shot spurts of blood from the severed ends of arteries. They worried that if they picked me up face down, as I still lay on the board, they might force the ragged ends of ribs into other organs and do further injury to me. Instead they rolled me onto my back, face up, and grabbed arms and legs to lift me off the board. Fighting their way through shallow water and surf, the three tried their best to keep both my body and head above the water. Everyone worried with each step that the shark might attack again.

I had remained fully conscious since the shark's first savage onslaught, but I now felt myself slipping, beginning to drift into unconsciousness, sure that I was dying and had no chance to survive. Al and Josh had each grabbed an arm, but Jack, who was holding my legs, had not stopped to take off his surf leash, and was dragging his board through the water behind him. When the fin dug in and caught, it tripped him and he stumbled. He lost his grip on my legs, causing everyone to stumble. My back whacked into the sand! He felt bad about it, but it may have saved my life. The jolt, like a slap in the face, brought me back to consciousness, reinvigorating my will to live. All I had wanted to do was to get to the beach before I died.

"Come on you guys," I thought to myself. "Take it easy, be gentle. I'm hurt bad."

I was again conscious, aware of Jack reaching down to undo the leash from his ankle, then again grabbing my other leg. The three lifted me above the water and struggled to get me onto the dry sand, where they laid me on my right side.

Watching the entire episode from a big house perched on top of the cliff above Haystack Rock was Dallas McKennon, a movie actor. He had been checking out the surf through binoculars when he noticed three men struggling through the surf carrying what appeared to him to be an injured surfer. Fine-focusing his lenses he could see blood in the water around us. He felt the man they carried was either dead or very badly injured. Realizing something serious had occurred, he dropped his glasses to the table, stepped around the blazing wood stove that warmed his house, grabbed the phone and dialed 9-1-1.

"Send an ambulance to the beach in front of Haystack Rock. It looks like a surfer has been badly injured." After hanging up, he rushed out his door and charged down the bluff.

In Seaside, 8 miles north, Sam, a local free-lance photographer, was in his darkroom developing a series of pictures he had taken of a lighthouse from a helicopter. As was his habit, he had his ER radio scanner on, keeping him in touch with potential news stories. He liked to get a head start on photographing events for the local papers. His ears perked up when he heard the caller excitedly request an ambulance and paramedics to aid an injured surfer on the beach near Haystack Rock. Within minutes he was driving south on Highway 101, his cameras and equipment, as always, carefully packed in the trunk of his car, ready for any emergency, or photographable event.

At about the same time the phone jangled in the usually quiet Cannon Beach Fire Department which housed the city ambulance and paramedic base station. It was on its third ring when Gary, one of the paramedics, shouted from the kitchen where he was preparing breakfast, "Hey, get the phone, please."

He was carrying two cups of steaming coffee when the excited voice of his partner stopped him in his tracks.

"No kidding!" exclaimed Jim, a look of shock on his face. "We're on our way."

He almost knocked the coffee cups out of Gary's hands as he rushed to the ambulance and yanked open the driver's door. The engine roared. The ambulance was already moving when Gary jumped in.

Ray, the relief paramedic, was digging clams along the beach about a mile south of Haystack rock when his belt beeper went off. He had just dug a gigantic razor clam from the wet sand. Shaking his head at the annoying interruption, he dropped it into the clam sack and raced across the sand to his truck where he radioed for a report. Shaking his head in disbelief he jumped in his rig and proceeded to the scene a mile north.

In the meantime, unaware the Dallas had already phoned for help, Steve, one of the surfers, winded from running across the beach and up the bluff, pounded on the door of the first house he came to. It was the downstairs half of a duplex. When no one answered, he tried the door and found it locked. He raced upstairs to the second-story apartment. Again no one answered his knock, but he could see a wall phone through the open curtains of a window. A big dog was standing in the middle of the room barking up a storm!

Frantic, he tried the door handle and found it unlocked. Entering slowly, he stared into the fangs of the growling dog. Scared, with hair standing up on the back of his neck, he walked sidewise past the dog, which continued to growl as he backed to where the phone was. Staring the dog down, Steve reached out and grabbed the phone. He was too excited to remember 9-1-1, so dialed O instead for the operator.

"May I help you?" the operator asked, in a casual voice.

"Quick, send an ambulance down to Haystack Rock in Cannon beach," he gasped.

"You must dial 9-1-1 for an emergency."

"Please do it for me," Steve pleaded, his hand shaking so badly he could not possibly dial. Also, his hands were still numb from surfing in the frigid water. "My friend has just been attacked by a giant shark, and there's a dog in here ready to chew me up!"

"A shark attack?" she said, this time in a voice that shook.

"Yes. Kenny Doudt," Steve's voice was rising as he was still gasping for breath from his long run.

"Just settle down," the operator said in a calming voice. "I'll notify the paramedics immediately."

"Thanks." Steve dropped the phone in its cradle, still staring into the intimidating eyes of the growling dog. He backed toward the door. Tripping over a throw rug, he stumbled and almost fell down. The dog lunged, his mouth snapping shut less than an inch from Steve's arm. Stepping quickly through the door, he slammed it on the dog just as it made its second lunge. He could see it through the window as it barked and clawed the inside of the door. As he rushed down the steps, he could still hear the dog frantically scratching and barking as he ran to his truck. He raced to the fire station to make sure help was on its way.

Gary maneuvered the speeding ambulance through the cars along the road, red lights flashing, siren screaming. An operator came on the radio, her voice excited as she informed them that the emergency was a shark attack at Haystack Rock.

"Jesus Christ!" Gary said reaching over to turn up the volume on the siren. "Did you hear that?"

He accelerated the medic wagon to maximum speed, still weaving in and out of traffic.

Steve, seeing and hearing the racing paramedics, flashed his lights and honked his horn to get their attention. He shouted out his open window and pointed down at Haystack Rock. He saw Gary nod in acknowledgment, then slow the ambulance for the turn down the beach.

Steve almost caused an accident when he made a U-turn in front of oncoming traffic, his tires spewing gravel as he fishtailed back onto the road, racing after the ambulance. Then he almost rammed into it when it slowed for a curve in the access above the sand. He was breathing in gasps, tears blinding his eyes, his stomach knotted with fear that his friend might already be dead. He could not believe anyone could live after being so badly mauled.

Sam, the photographer, heard the same emergency call that the ambulance heard—a surfer near Haystack Rock had been attacked by a shark. Sucking in his breath he increased his speed, wishing he had a siren as he met the traffic in Cannon Beach. He had been successfully selling photographs to local papers and magazines, but to be the first on the scene of a shark attack incident might get his pictures onto UPI or even on television.

As I lay on my side before the medics arrived, I felt increasing pain with each breath, making it impossible not to moan. My obvious increasing pain scared Jack, who ran off for help, leaving me in Josh's care. It had been a couple of minutes since they carried me from the water, but to Josh it seemed liked hours. I could hear him praying out loud as he held me on my side, begging God to let me live.

I was still on my side when Tom and Mike's car skidded to a stop not 10 feet from where I lay. Josh, his skin ashen, tried valiantly to hold the torn flaps of flesh closed over the wounds, hoping to slow the bleeding. He was still praying, with Tom and Mike now at his side. Tom looked at Mike after seeing the blood ooze from between Josh's fingers.

They felt there was no way I could survive. The sand beneath me was already soaked with blood from the gaping wound which ran the length of my back.

Tom and Mike stared out into the ocean expecting once again to see a dorsal fin appear above the surface.

Tom knelt beside Josh using both of his hands to help hold the wound closed, Mike, seeing there was little he could do, ran to his car for a towel. The used ones Josh had were already soaked with blood. They covered my wound, then leaned close to my ear telling me, "Hang in there, bro. You're gonna make it."

"You're gonna be okay, Kenny," Josh sobbed. "I know you are."

Tom took hold of my gloved hand, rubbing the skin to warm it. He then rubbed my legs and arms through the wet suit, hoping that would keep me from going into shock.

"Tom," I whispered. "Please take off my gloves."

Tom started to do as I had asked, then stopped, deciding they would help keep me warmer. Even though they were all sure I was dying, they worked their hardest to keep me as warm and comfortable as possible for what they thought were the last few minutes of my life. They could hear me mumble, but they were unable to understand what I was trying to say. Everyone was surprised I was still conscious and talking.

Josh was unaware of the crowd that had gathered. People pressed in close to get a better look at my wounds. One of those gathered was Mike's girlfriend, a registered nurse. She took one look at me, and shook her head without much hope, "The best thing we can do for him is to keep him warm. Does anyone have a blanket?"

"Yeah, we do," said a young lady, who grabbed her boyfriend's arm and ran down the beach to get it. They returned a minute later carrying an old army blanket.

"Hold it up to break the wind," ordered the R.N. An icy wind was whipping across the sand, raising goose bumps on those standing there watching.

"May I be of assistance?" a tourist inquired.

"Sure," answered Steve, handing him a corner of the blanket used to shield me from the wind. He took it and inquisitively lowered one corner to take a peek at my wounds. Looking down on the torn and bleeding flesh and protruding ribs, he dropped the blanket, fell to his knees, vomiting uncontrollably, until someone helped him to his feet and away from the scene.

I tried to block out the terrible pain which engulfed my body by thinking of my sons, Jeremy and Justin. I knew that if I did not fight to live, I would never see them again. The distant scream of a siren raised my spirits. There was no way I was going to give up. I had to see my boys again, and tell them how much I loved them. I had too much to live for to let go.

"Slow down, Gary!" Jim shouted over the scream of the siren.

"I hope it's been cleared," Gary said slowing the ambulance down to enter the beach access. "I saw some people stuck a couple of days ago."

"We may have to use four wheel drive," Jim suggested.

"No, it looks like it's been cleared." Gary let the ambulance roll through, then speeded up when he got on the flat hard packed sand. "It's hard to believe a guy could get attacked by a shark so far north. I guess it's all the rain and heavy river runoff, and maybe there was a school of steelhead offshore, still in school."

"Who knows?" Jim said pointing, ahead toward the people who were crowded around me. "The poor guy was in the wrong place at the wrong time, or maybe the right place at the wrong time, I don't know."

"Man!" Jim exclaimed. "Look at the size of that crowd already gathered."

"It's a good thing other surfers were out to help him."

"I'm going to honk the horn."

The crowd slowly divided, for the ambulance, leaving only a narrow lane, Gary jammed his hand down on the horn, hitting one last blast on the siren at the same time.

My spirits rose when I heard the siren get louder and louder. I felt, when I heard the tires slapping across the hard packed sand and the crowd grow quiet, that I might make it after all. I had come to the conclusion that the only think keeping me alive were my eyes, I thought that if I let them close, I would never open them again. I began to feel safe when the ambulance stopped close to where I lay.

Both paramedics were surprised when Sam aimed his camera at them. He caught them again as they pulled the stretcher out of the back and set it on the sand beside me.

"How'd Sam get here so quick?" mumbled Gary as he leaned down to fold back the sheet covering the stretcher.

"You know Sam," Jim answered. "He always has his emergency scanner on, even when he's taking a shower." Jim, looking back up from the stretcher grinning, shouted at the crowd, "Please move back. We need more room."

The crowd moved quickly.

Gary dropped to his knees, setting the already opened first aid kit next to me. Josh, still holding me, explained to Gary what had just happened. Concerned, he pulled aside the blood-soaked towel covering the gaping wounds. The crowd gasped when they saw the wounds, but again pressed close, leaning over the medics to get a closer look. Gary shook his head as he moved his fingers up and down my arm trying to find a pulse.

"We gotta get him to the hospital quick, and I mean quick!" Gary said, helping Jim to slide me onto the stretcher. Again Sam's camera went off in their faces.

"How about moving your head so I can get a close-up of the wound?" Sam asked, almost tripping Gary as he stepped around him.

"We've got a guy dying, and you want him to pose for pictures!"

They told Sam to back off out of the way. They moved the stretcher around to work on me. Nevertheless, he continued to take pictures.

By that time, Ray, a third paramedic, had arrived and immediately joined in trying to keep me alive. The first thing they did was to set up a nasal cannula for administration.

"How's his blood pressure?"

"What pressure?" "There is no pressure, the pulse is thready and barely palpable."

"I can't believe he's still alive."

"Hypothermia." He answered.

"His body temperature has dropped below ninety degrees."

"Pulse is weak and very irregular. We gotta get blood into this guy and get him warmed up. Otherwise he'll arrest."

Hearing the paramedics discuss my wounds and what they needed to do didn't bother me until I heard my suit being cut off. It was worth a good $250.

"Get some blankets out and let's get this guy warmed up."

I could do nothing but listen. The slicing off of my wet suit worried me more about how much it had cost than I was afraid about losing my life. The suit was only a couple of months old, but at least thinking about it kept my mind off of dying. I could not tell who said it, but I heard a voice say, "Stick in an I.V."

Next I felt myself being lifted as they pulled my wet suit from beneath, then a coolness as my wounds became exposed. The next sensation was a slight pressure around my torso when the paramedics placed trauma dressings over the area to protect me and slow the bleeding. My legs were lifted onto the MAST trousers. They closed the Velcro around my legs. I felt the pressure on my legs as they pumped them up, which allowed what remaining blood I had to be more available to my vital organs. By then, I was covered with blankets to help retain my body heat.

The medics were annoyed by Sam and his camera as they lifted the stretcher into the ambulance.

"Jesus," Ray said. "Come on, don't take any more pictures."

Sam moved back, then leaned around to get a last shot before the back door closed. He took a last look at the back of the ambulance, then cocked his camera and turned to Steve and Jack, hoping to get some more pictures while he had them on the beach.

Jim jumped in and started the engine while Gary and Ray got into the back to work on keeping me alive, a task they both thought hopeless. One or the other kept asking me questions, trying to keep me alert while checking the I.V., tubes, oxygen, and monitoring equipment. Jim steered the vehicle back across the sand and up the access to the main road with the siren screaming.

The paramedics had barely pulled away when Sam turned to Steve and Jack asking them what had happened.

"Listen," Jack said. "We gotta get to the hospital. Josh and Al are already on their way."

"Do me a favor," Sam asked. "Can I take some photos? I need one of Kenny's board. Can you hold it up for me please? I want to get a picture of the bite marks. Maybe I can take the board back to my lab and get some close-ups."

Sam started to walk over to Jack and Steve. Jack said, "The board is mine and Kenny just borrowed it for this morning session."

Sam began snapping pictures of them pointing out to sea, holding up the board and looking at the bite marks.

"How about one more, for the press," said Sam lifting his camera to his eye and fiddling with the fine focus.

"That's enough!" Jack said. "He was our good friend."

Sam shrugged as he shot a couple of last pictures of Jack and Steve collecting the pieces of the wet suit off the sand.

"Hey, you guys," shouted Sam as they left. "Hope you aren't mad.

I'm just doing my job. The media will be clamoring for pictures. I feel bad about Kenny getting bitten too."

Steve and Jack acknowledged Sam's explanation, then trotted across the sand to Steve's car.

People still stood on the beach talking about the attack, some pointing out to sea, others searching the surface, expecting to see a dorsal fin. All were relieved they had not been in the water when the attack had occurred. Sam snapped off a few shots of the crowd and of Haystack Rock. Satisfied, he ran to his car. His hope was to get the film developed as quickly as possible, then drive the pictures to Portland. He was sure that the press would pay to buy everything he had.

In the meantime, the ambulance roared through the streets of Cannon Beach, the siren screaming, cars pulling over to get out of the way, people leaning out of windows and doorways to see what the noise was all about.

Jim grabbed the radio microphone and called ahead to warn the Seaside Hospital emergency staff to get prepared for a major trauma. "We've got a surfer who has been badly mauled by a large shark in the ocean off Haystack Rock."

"Yeah, okay we'll be ready for him." Jim looked at Ray and said, "I don't think she takes us seriously!"

Continuing on the radio, Jim said, "This is for real. The victim has a deep laceration on the left side of his body running from just below his armpit to the middle of his buttocks, extending across his back almost to his spine. There is also a major laceration across his left buttock. That's how deep the laceration is. He has lost most of his blood. You can see his ribs. His flesh is laid back in a 4 to 6-inch strip. This guy is in real bad shape!"

Jim could feel himself getting excited, his voice rising several decibels with each sentence.

"Just have the ER ready! His vitals are poor. You'll need lots of blood. He can't have much left and he's still losing it."

Although I could hear them talking, I had begun to feel I was going to make it. Being in the hands of the paramedics gave me faith that I would live. I still could not believe what had happened to me. There was not great pain, just a feeling of weakness. The only uncomfortable sensation was the terrific cold throughout my body.

Growing weaker, having lost at least six pints of blood and suffering from extreme hypothermia, I was barely aware of the paramedics working on me. Cold permeated every portion of my body. As uncomfortable as the cold made me, I later learned that it was the hypothermia that slowed down my bodily functions, a major reason why I am still alive.

The ambulance ride to Seaside Hospital seemed so fast. My only annoyance was the continual and repetitious questioning by the paramedics. They would ask my name, then how I spelled it. Next they would ask my age, my weight, my address, the names of my kids, my friends. As soon as I got through that, they would start again. Then, without warning, the siren went silent, making me apprehensive that my end was near. I calmed down when I finally realized we were at the hospital and the ambulance was backing up to the ER entrance.

The next thing I remembered was seeing the ambulance door being yanked open. The head doctor of the emergency room appeared and immediately began barking out orders. Paramedics, uniformed nurses and orderlies rushed about doing his bidding. I felt a jolt as paramedics slid the stretcher out and dropped its wheels to the concrete. Since I could feel and hear things happening, I knew I was still alive. I was aware of being rolled down the hallway, people rushing along beside me holding up bottles attached to rubber tubes to various parts of my body.

"Somebody get a sample of his blood so we can cross-match it," I heard the ER doctor order.

Almost immediately a needle was inserted into one of my veins. The nurse began to worry when it took so long to fill the syringe. Dr. Wayne was now being paged over the loudspeaker ordering him to the emergency room.

"He is in the middle of a double hernia operation." A nurse said. "It will be several minutes before he is finished in the operating room."

The ER doctor cracked out an order that the carpet layer who had cut off two fingers would have to be moved out of the ER to make room for me.

"There's nothing that can be done for him anyway until his partner returns with the cut-off fingers," said a voice.

The poor man was disturbed at being forced to vacate the operating table until he caught sight of my torn back as they wheeled me in. A nurse told him "Look at this guy, and it might help the pain you're in."

I was beginning to feel severe pain in several places and I was becoming worried at the apparent confusion in the emergency room. I could hear blaring orders for more supplies and equipment. Requests were made for more medical help. I felt a nurse insert a new I.V. so they could pump blood back in my still bleeding body. It was either replace the blood faster than it was running out or there was no chance I could be saved.

"Try to relax," I heard the ER doctor say. "I'm going to insert a chest tube into your lung to make your breathing easier."

I relaxed as best I could, feeling something press into my rib cage, the pressure repeated again before the doctor succeeded in getting the tube between my ribs into my left lung.

Finally Dr. Wayne had another doctor relieve him on the double hernia operation and rushed to the emergency room where most of the nurses and the emergency room doctor were covered with my blood which continued to seep and spurt from a dozen puncture wounds. The blood transfusions were barely able to keep up with the loss.

I was still conscious and starting to feel more pain. Then I caught sight of Steve's girlfriend, Suzi, peeking over the shoulder of one of the nurses to see how I was. She worked at the hospital, but the expression on her face was pure shock and horror when she looked down at my back in total disbelief. Her hand moved involuntarily to her mouth as she staggered backward.

More nurses rushed in carrying bundles of clean gauze, while others rushed out with blood-soaked one. A nurse entered with liter bottles of fluids on a tray. Blood was on the way to replace that which dripped from my wounds onto the operating table, then onto the floor.

Two orderlies helped Dr. Wayne roll me from my back onto my right side, exposing gashes and wounds. The doctor's voice showed his noticeable alarm as he stepped back from the table and said, "Get the

Coast Guard on the phone immediately. We have to move this man to a Portland Hospital. There is no way we can handle this severe a case with the limited equipment we have here."

Within minutes a nurse rushed into the ER to say, "The Coast Guard says their helicopter would not be able to make it from Astoria to Portland. There's a major storm over the coastal range."

"Then get an ambulance for us," Dr. Wayne said. "See that there is ample blood for continuing transfusion. The pressure on the MAST trousers will have to be kept high. He is still losing blood almost as fast as we can get it into him."

Nurses, orderlies, and emergency room personnel rushed about following the doctor's orders, all knowing that saving my life was down to mere seconds of times. I felt myself lifted back onto a gurney, then pushed out of the emergency room and down a brightly lit corridor. While the double doors were held open two orderlies rushed me outside. A rush of cold air hit my face just before the paramedics and Dr. Wayne slid me back into the ambulance. I head the roar of the engine and the tug of speed on my body as we moved forward. I began to worry there was no way we could make it in time.

The driver turned on the siren and accelerated away from the Seaside Hospital, beginning what would be a long tortuous drive through the coastal mountain ranges to Portland.

"It sure is a beautiful day," the driver said as he hit the siren and slowed for an intersection. "I never get tired of looking at the ocean."

Dr. Wayne ignored the observation as he bent close to examine the oxygen mask over my face. I was having a hard time breathing, which worried him. After taking it off and checking the air intake, he replaced it.

"Look at all the people lining the streets," the driver said blasting the siren again. "Everyone in Seaside must have heard about the attack."

"If they want gore," the paramedic said, "they ought to go see the emergency room. There was blood everywhere—on the walls, on the floor, on the examining table."

"It's coming over the radio stations now," the driver said turning up the volume, an announcer describing the attack. He estimated the shark to be more than 15 feet long.

I could barely understand the discussion inside the ambulance when Dr. Wayne shook my shoulder and asked, "What's your name?" He didn't want me to close my eyes.

I heard the doctor complain that he was having a hard time getting blood into my body fast enough to keep up with the blood I was still losing.

"How are you feeling?" Dr. Wayne asked again, shaking my shoulder. "Hang on, buddy, we'll be in Portland in a little while."

I knew he was trying to keep my spirits up and keep me alert. Every time I blinked, he would check the air intake from the oxygen tank. The ambulance had to keep slowing as it went around sharp mountain curves. The snow was falling faster. The wheels kept spinning on the ice each time the driver tried to accelerate around a hairpin curve. The ambulance slowed down, then stopped.

"It looks like there's been a wreck up ahead," his assistant said. "A car is upside down, partially blocking the road."

We started moving again when a bystander waved us around the wrecked car. The siren screamed the entire time as we bumped along the side of the road to get past.

"There's a bad wreck on Highway 26 about 40 miles west of Portland," the driver said into the radio mike. "Better get another ambulance and the highway patrol here quick."

I felt as though I was traveling through a fairyland, with everything white outside the window I looked through. The ambulance lights spread red color across the snow. Every time I closed my eyes and began to think about my sons, the doctor would shake me and ask questions to see if I was still conscious.

The doctor reached across me to adjust the intravenous tubing, chest tubes and monitoring electrodes.

"His blood pressure has dropped to zero," I heard him say.

I could tell he was worried, but to me everything was peaceful, like I was floating up to heaven. There was no pain, only a little numbness. I was full of faith that Dr. Wayne could keep me alive.

It's hard to explain my life flashing before my eyes, but oddly enough, it did happen. It was sort of like watching parts of my life on a television screen. I saw the time I almost drowned when I was only two years old, in the ocean off New Jersey, and then everything since. The part of my life that kept floating through my mind was recollections of my sons, Justin and Jeremy. I had to live, or I would never see them again.

Dr. Wayne kept shaking me out of my dream world with more questions. I could tell he was concerned by the way he kept monitoring my pulse and blood pressure. He kept increasing the pressure in the MAST trousers to force what blood I had left up from my legs into my upper torso and brain. When my pulse increased and my blood pressure began to rise he seemed to relax a bit.

Actually, it was very peaceful, staring out the window at the white snow banks passing by. It was so serene that I really did not worry about how precarious my life was.

"How much further?" I heard Dr. Wayne ask the driver.

"We're almost out of the mountains now," he answered.

"Which hospital do you want me to head for?"

"How long is it to St. Vincent?" the doctor asked.

"Between fifteen and twenty minutes."

"Radio them that we are on our way," the doctor ordered.

I was starting to fade away again, having a hard time keeping my mind focused or my eyes open. Dr. Wayne immediately pumped more pressure into the MAST trousers, continually assuring me that I would be all right.

"We're almost at St. Vincent," I heard the driver say. "Is he gonna make it?"

"He's got to! We're too close, and he's held on for so long."

The driver cranked the siren up a few more notches and seemed to step on the gas. The ambulance was flying down the highway. I felt the ambulance turn off the highway. It then went down under an overpass to the entrance of the hospital emergency room. Doctors, nurses, and orderlies were waiting in the open doorway as the ambulance backed up to the entrance. The back door was yanked open and a rush of cold air hit me as they lifted me out, lowered the wheels on the gurney and rolled me into the hospital.

"Hang in there," Dr. Wayne said into my ear. "We made it."

I was sure that the doctors, paramedics, and nurses had done everything they could to keep me alive up to this point. Now it would be up to the surgeons to put me back together.

As they rolled me down the hall, a surgeon named Dr. Starr leaned over me examining the wounds and at the same time telling me I was going to be all right.

"We are going to lift you onto the operating table," Dr. Starr said. "The nurse will give you a shot to relieve the pain."

He then grabbed my arm and moved it, mumbling something I could not understand. I was in pain. It was the first major pain I had felt because my body was warming up.

"Don't move me," I begged, tears running down my face.

"Nurse," Dr. Starr said. "Give him the shot now."

I could feel the needle slide into my arm, lessening the pain almost immediately. My life was in the absolute control of the doctors surrounding the operating table. I no longer worried, trusting in the doctors as if they were God.

The operating room had been put in full readiness for my arrival, a top surgical team of six doctors scrubbed, gowned, and ready to go. Doctors Ahmad, Ham, Okubo, Matsui, Egan, and Starr were highly trained for open-heart surgery. Lucky me!

I could hear the commotion, but everything seemed to be happening in slow motion now and in muted tones. I could barely make out the figures clustered around the operating table, their voices distorted, as I slipped into unconsciousness.

I had immediately been connected to monitoring devices, screens showing all my vital signs for the doctors to read as they worked.

Once they had my vital signs under control, they examined my back and buttocks. A photographer aimed his camera at the wounds and took pictures for a medical journal. He took one shot with a doctor holding up a slab of flesh showing the gravity of the wound.

Everyone went to work. The first stage of the operation was an exploration of my left chest cavity. Next came wound repair by surgeons Ahmad, Ham, Okubo, and Matsui. The wound consisted of a gaping hole, a collapsed lung, and four fractured ribs. The ribs had been broken in several places and some were splintered by the shark's teeth. My back muscles hung loosely around the wound cavity and there was massive bleeding into the left lung.

After a thorough examination of the lung, heart, and left hemidiaphragm, or kidney, they found no significant damage to any of those organs. The skin around the chest wound had been serrated by the shark's teeth and some of the muscles were missing.

Next, four broken ribs were rejoined. Before they could complete the repair of the ribs, the bleeding had to be brought under control. The collapsed lung was re-expanded by repairing the broken ribs and chest wall. The bleeding arteries in the muscles overlying the torn ribs were ligated. Then the soft tissue was put in place and stitched up. Drainage tubes were left in place and connected to an underwater seal.

At this stage, the lacerations were left to Dr. Starr to repair.

The doctors participating in the next phase of the surgery were Starr, Ahmad, Ham, and Okubo. In their examination they found a jagged laceration on the left side of my torso, passing in a ragged, irregular line posteriorly and downward. The total length of this wound was approximately 14 inches. Just distal to that wound was a second such laceration of about 7 inches in length.

Both wounds required considerable undermining for closure. They were deep enough to sever a portion of the *latissimus dorsi*—the main back muscle. Both wounds were repaired by Dr. Ahmad.

There was a third massive wound which was a 10-inch long, V-shaped flap based, on the lateral aspect of the left buttocks. This wound was deep enough to lacerate the *gluteus maximus* and several fragments of that muscle, as well as chunk of subcutaneous fat, were missing. All of the wounds contained what appeared to be sand, but no other foreign material.

After the chest wound had been closed by Dr. Ahmad, I was placed on my right side, and the affected areas were prepared with Betadine.

Debridement of the wound edges was carried out with a number 20 scalpel and deep closure performed with a number 4-0 Vicryl. The skin was closed by interrupted ethilon. A large soft rubber Penrose drain was inserted beneath each of the three separate wounds, three on the wound on the buttock. In addition, a hemovac suction tube was inserted under the lacerated portion of the *gluteus maximus.* Any muscle or subcutaneous fat with questionable viability was excised. Before closing, all wounds had been repeatedly irrigated with saline solution and cleaned with 4 x 4 gauze pads. At the completion of wound closures, the operative sites were covered with xeroform gauze, followed by 4 x 4 pads, fluffs, ABDs, and Kerlix dressings.

In summary, I had suffered severe damage to four ribs smashed by the power of the shark's teeth and jaws. The monster had exerted a force of approximately 15,000 pounds per square inch in its bite. In addition, I had a punctured lung, exposed heart and kidney, shredded muscles, severed nerves, mutilation of fatty tissue, and massive internal bleeding.

I had lost all but one pint of the eleven pints of blood a body generally holds. My body temperature had dropped below ninety degrees Fahrenheit, but ironically, it was the extreme hypothermia that slowed down all my bodily functions and probably saved my life.

The shark had inflicted a half-pie-shaped wound that went from just below my armpit to the middle of my left side. According to the doctors, if the teeth had gone another half inch further toward my backbone, the spinal cord could have been severed, paralyzing me from there on down. Dr. Starr quit counting the stitches when he reached five hundred. Fortunately, they said I was in good enough shape that my body tolerated all these procedures well.

Once I was in stable enough condition to be moved, I was taken to intensive care. It had taken more than three hours of surgery to complete the repairs on my back and inside my chest. The doctors gathered in a room for a press conference that afternoon, before media representatives from all over the northwest.

In the meantime, back at Cannon Beach, the local media were covering the reaction of the residents to the attack. There was a big crowd just off the beach, which was not only a popular surf spot, but well known to residents and tourists alike. People had gathered to talk in the Round Table, one of the town's more popular restaurants. It got its name from the gigantic round table in the middle of the dining room which could seat twenty or more people.

None of the locals who gathered were yet ready to accept the reality of a shark attack at their beach. Most believed I had banged into a rock. Others agreed with the people on the beach just after the attack, who had said it was an angered sea lion.

Two guys who surfed got up and looked out the window, a look of worry on their faces. Neither was sure he would ever want to surf there again.

November 28, 1979, the first day after the attack, I was so deeply under sedation that Dr. Ahmad had a nurse give me a shot to bring me out of it. He and the crew stood around my bed watching for signs of consciousness.

With the realization of what had been done to save me, I realized I could have been dead.

Although I was happy to be alive, pain throbbed throughout my entire body with each heartbeat, from the tips of my fingers to the ends of my toes. I really wasn't sure where I was or what had happened to me.

I hurt so badly, my body shook uncontrollably, as if I was freezing. I tried to twist around to escape the pain, but I was strapped to my bed.

Relief came when the nurse gave me a shot of morphine. The pain began to fade away almost instantly. So did my mind, which drifted off into space.

I was aware, as I lay strapped to my bed, of the clicking noise of the life support system I was hooked up to, with small screens, dials, and instrument banks stacked behind me. When I looked down at myself to see if I still had my arms and legs, all I could see were tubes connected to every part of my body. Needles were stuck into my skin in what seemed to me to be every available bit of space.

As I became more aware of what was going on, I found that I had made the front page of newspapers all over the northwest. No one had ever survived so savage an attack by a Great White Shark. I was also told that the doctors held a press conference. Television crews came in from

Portland and Seattle. Other crews headed out over the ocean at Cannon Beach, hoping to spice up their stories with sightings of the shark.

Terry Link, a local fish and wildlife expert from Astoria, Oregon, arrived at Cannon Beach to examine the jaw print in the surfboard. He needed to find teeth or fragments of a tooth to make a positive identification of the type of shark that had attacked me. He was unable to find even one fragment on the surface, so he had the board taken to Oregon State University to be radiographed. Through that method, they were able to discover one small tooth fragment a quarter of an inch long. From that they were able to make a positive identification that it had been a Great White, whose scientific name is *Carcharodon carcharias.*

The remainder of the day I lay in my bed, so heavily sedated I did not realize where I was or event that I was alive. By the second day excellent care had stabilized my condition. However, every time the morphine wore off, the pain would again tear through my body. I'd never hurt so badly in my life. Sharp pains stabbed into every portion of my legs, arms, fingers, toes, chest, stomach—you name it!

When I started to moan and groan and twist about in the bed, nurses, who seldom left my side, injected morphine into the I.V. which was inserted into a vein in my arm. When the morphine entered my blood stream, it was such a wonderful relief from the pain. My eyes would roll back and I would drift off into space. They kept me heavily sedated through the second day, although, by the end of that day, I had begun to become aware of things going on around me and of my body.

Dr. Ahmad stopped by my bed during his evening rounds, holding my arm while he explained that I had survived an attack by a shark. He read the fear in my mind as my eyes focused on the many dials and screens connected to my body with tubes and wires. He carefully explained the use of each. Then I again drifted off into sleep, not remembering what he said, or much else about those first two days in cardiac recovery.

It sure made me realize how easily a person could get hooked on drugs. The sedation kept me floating in a wonderful but illusory world of no worries, pain or apprehension.

By the third day I surprised the medical staff with the remarkable recovery I had been making. They unstrapped me and allowed me to sit up in bed. My ex-wife and friends were allowed to visit. The doctors let me watch television. I seem to recall it was a football game. However, what really happened the third day is still a bit vague, because a couple of different times I was given shots of morphine to control the pain.

Later that night I awoke to find myself alone. I did not know where I was or what had happened. I was not even sure who I was. I was sweating so badly, that my bed and covers were soaked. I was so scared I began to shake. It was most likely from coming down off the morphine. When a nurse came in to check on me, I grabbed her and held her close, to make sure I was still alive. I had to hold on to something real. After that, I was given less and less morphine.

On the morning of the fourth day, they removed all tubes and wires from my body. For the first time since the attack, I was free to move my arms and legs. I was just getting used to my new freedom of movement when a nurse stopped by my bed to tell me about a four-year-old boy, also in cardiac recovery, who had just had open-heart surgery and was lonely and scared. His bed was only a few down from mine and she thought maybe if I talked with him, I could cheer him up.

If felt good to be able to do something for someone else. I pushed myself up into a sitting position, then got to my feet. I picked up a surfing magazine one of my buddies had left me and walked the short distance over to his bed.

He seemed to pep up when I sat down on the side of his bed and went through the magazine, showing him photos of guys surfing big waves. His eyes got really wide as I described my experience to him. I lifted my gown to show him the stitched scars running the length of my back. I was amazed at how well he was taking his own operation. I had to fight back tears when he asked me if I was going to be all right. A nurse stopped by later and thanked me for cheering him up.

Later that day, Dr. Ahmad looked in on me again and said I was recovering very well and that I was to be moved from cardiac recovery to another room the following morning. I sort of hated to leave the recovery ward. I had certainly received special treatment.

The next morning I was placed in a wheelchair and moved to a private room on the seventh floor. The hospital's public relations official stopped by to tell me that every television news channel and newspaper in the state wanted to interview me. Dr. Ahmad said that it would be all right, but he wanted me to rest for a couple more days so that I could get my thoughts together before facing reporters. Only my close friends were allowed to visit.

The hospital photographer came by to visit and gave me some pictures he had taken during the operation. He went over each photo, describing what had happened and what was done by the surgical team. I was shocked, totally unable to believe that what I was seeing were pictures of myself. That same day a friend brought me a book about sharks. I had always known about sharks and worried about them to some extent while surfing, but with the book, I really began to learn about them.

An elementary teacher from a nearby kindergarten class came by to give me 18-by-12-inch get-well cards her students had drawn for me. I still treasure each of the many get-well cards I received while I was in the hospital and I received literally dozens. I did not know there were so many wonderful caring people.

On the third day after I moved to my new room, reporters began to drop by to interview me for the local television news channels. The media people were actually lined up outside my door and down the hallway. Only one reporter was allowed into my room at a time.

In addition to the reporters who came to my room, I got phone calls from all over the country. The *National Enquirer* sent a beautiful lady all the way to Oregon from the east coast to write a story about me. She stayed around for several days and treated me with special kindness. It was great!

I recall one of the days I was all alone, lying on the bed looking through the photos of my wounds which were taken during the surgery. That's when the reality of it all really hit me hard. I had come so close to death and I could not deny the mental trauma the attack caused. The next thing I knew I was crying uncontrollably.

From then on, every day there was someone who wanted to do a story about the attack and my recovery. If I didn't feel up to it the nurses would turn them away, telling them to come back later when I felt better. I don't think anybody ever was treated better than me. I really felt such concern and real caring from all the hospital staff.

A day or so later a doctor came in to remove my stitches. He had me lie on my stomach, then started snipping and pulling out the stitches that had held me together. I had a strange sensation when I turned my head to watch him pull the thread from my back. I must admit, it worried me that I might open up again if I moved.

Dr. Ahmad told me I should exercise my left arm as soon as possible. At first it not only worried me to move it too much, but it hurt. However, I did as I was told, lifting it, then holding it straight out from my body. I would walk up and down the hallway, lifting, then stretching my left arm. Most people, including the nurses and some of the doctors, could not believe I was already up and walking about.

Each day they cut down on the pain medication. Whatever they replaced the morphine with did not work as well. The pain began to set in with a dull throbbing sensation invading my body. I also had a stinging sensation in the tips of my fingers and toes. According to the doctors, this was caused by the nerve damage I had suffered. The sorest spot on my back was where the shark's teeth had scraped off layers of skin leaving it open and raw.

I was really surprised when Dr. Starr came to my room to inform me that I was to be released from the hospital the next morning. He attributed my remarkable recovery to my having been in such good shape from doing physical labor and from surfing. I didn't really want to leave. I had never been treated better in my life.

Since I did not have any clothes when I was admitted, Steve's girlfriend and his sister brought me new socks, tennis shoes, a sweat suit and a stocking cap with a "superman" sign on it.

My friend Potts, who lived in Portland, came by on the day of my release to take me to his home. Potts and I grew up together in Houston, Texas, and were good friends.

I had spent a total of eleven days in the hospital. Although I was happy to be alive, I was scared to face life on the outside, knowing it would be different than what I was used to.

As the nurse wheeled me to the exit, my friends surrounded me. One was carrying my surfboard, another the get-well cards and gifts people had given me. I realized as I went through the door and onto the street, that my time of being treated like royalty had come to an end. Gritting my teeth, I stood up, took my surfboard under my arm, and walked to the waiting car. It was then, again, that cold reality slapped me hard across the face. I realized I had been badly chewed up and spit out and I'd nearly lost my life!

BLACK DECEMBER

Tim Wallett

The blockbuster movie Jaws *brought into sharp focus the clash of entrepreneurs wanting to profit from the waterfront tourist trade and the sharks that occasionally attack the tourists. "Black December," set in South African waters, plays out this clash in bright red colors. The literature suggests such serial attacks occur cyclically—and for reasons still unknown.*

"Black December" began at 1700, December 18, 1957, at the resort of Karridene. Sixteen-year-old Robert Wherley, an amateur lifesaver, was bodysurfing 50 meters offshore in chest-deep water. He was situated slightly to the right of the bathing area so that he could avoid others while surfing. He had been in the water for about twenty minutes when he felt what he thought was a piece of seaweed brush his leg. Simultaneously he saw a shadow moving away from him. Discolored water obscured its form and Wherley did not recognize it until a shark's dorsal fin broke the surface.

"It was only then that I realized what was happening. I saw the shark coming at me and there was nothing I could do. I tried moving sideways but it was no good. There was this jarring shock as the shark grabbed my leg. I surged through the water as it swam with me in its mouth."

Terror struck, Wherley punched at the shark and tried to hit its snout. The shark shook him violently and as it bit through his leg he was free.

"As my head broke the surface I began to splash with my arms and scream for help," he recalls. "It was all I could do to chase the shark away. Then I became aware of blood in the water around me. I realized for the first time that I must be hurt. I saw a wave building and tried to bodysurf to shore. My legs felt strange and I lost the wave after riding it a short distance. I was trying to stand when two tourists came to help me."

Hundreds of people gasped at the horrific sight as Wherley was carried onto the beach. His left leg had been bitten off at the knee and blood poured from the stump. After administering first-aid the unconscious youth was transported to hospital where his life hung in the balance for many hours. By the following day he had improved slightly but was still in a critical condition. Expert medical treatment ensured his complete recovery in three months.

The evening Wherley lost his leg nobody could have foreseen the horror which was to follow. The next day hundreds of people went back into the sea in the area where the incident had taken place.

Two days later, at 1600 on Friday, December 20, 1957, a second attack took place at Uvongo.

Allan Green, fifteen-years-old, was standing on a sandbank 30 meters from shore. A deep channel separated the sandbank from the beach. About forty other bathers had crossed this channel and were being buffeted by the 1.2 meter waves breaking on the back. A cry for help suddenly punctuated the sound of the surf. Eyewitnesses describe how Allan Green was pushed backwards through the surf and a large shark's tail broke the surface and began "lashing the water." A number of bathers began scrambling toward the beach while others stood horrorstruck, watching the feebly struggling young man as the waves broke over him. They soon realized that the shark had left the scene and two bathers went to his assistance.

A human chain was formed across the channel and laboriously the boy was pulled to shore. By the time he reached the safety of dry land he was dead.

The mass of onlookers looked disbelievingly at the remains of Green's mutilated right arm and the gaping wounds bitten into his chest and stomach. When the ambulance arrived twenty minutes later the sea was deserted.

Newspapers, utilizing the sensational value of shark attack, made full use of this incident. Tourists viewed the occurrence with apprehension and a number of families decided to return home.

Three days later twenty-three-year-old Vernon Berry arrived in Margate at 1300 for a five-day visit before proceeding to Cape Town where he was to compete in a motorcycle race. At 1600 that same day he and two friends joined about a hundred people in the bathing area. Shortly afterwards a group of African men, about 300 meters north of the main beach, saw a large shark swimming toward the bathers. One of the men began running down the beach shouting a warning as he went. A tourist, sitting on a clump of rocks overlooking the bathing area, saw the shark approaching Berry. He stood up and shouted "Shark!" but realized immediately his warning was too late. At that moment the shark tore into the body of its victim and pushed him along the surface.

One of Berry's friends heard the warning shout and turned to see Berry wide-eyed, ploughing sideways through a breaking wave. Shark and victim then began to turn grotesque somersaults in the waist-deep water. As the shark completed its attack the two friends came to help Berry who was floundering helplessly on his back in a spreading stain of blood.

Berry was pulled to the water's edge and as he was lifted from the sea he exclaimed in horror "Oh my God! Just look at me!" and lost consciousness. His left forearm had been amputated, his right arm almost stripped of all flesh, his lower abdomen, buttocks, and right thigh had been bitten away. Berry never regained consciousness and died a short while later on the way to hospital.

What had started as a minor incident five days earlier now deteriorated into widespread panic as the entire Natal South Coast area became aware of an unseen menace which lurked behind the foaming breakers. At 0900 the following day a fund was opened to sponsor anti-shark measures at Uvongo Beach. Residents and visitors subscribed liberally to raising £400 (R800) by 1500 the same day. An emergency meeting was called by the Tuna Angling Club to discuss ways of catching sharks. Members undertook an intensive shark catching program in which they used kites to take their baits beyond the breakers. A Durham businessman put forward a plan to use four helicopters to patrol bathing beaches. Light aircraft flew low over the coast to spot sharks and warn bathers.

The ineffectiveness of spotter planes was proved at 1300 on December 30, 1957, when a fourteen-year-old girl, Julia Painting, was attacked moments after a spotter plane had passed over Margate's bathing area.

Julia, her fifteen-year-old nephew, an uncle and a friend, Paul Brokensha, had gone for a final swim before returning home to Rhodesia. The sea was clam with several hundred bathers packing the bathing area. The little group was standing about 50 meters offshore, slightly isolated from the crowd. Without warning, a shark appeared and made for Julia who was standing in waist-deep water. With a savage thrust it tore out a portion of her left buttock, pulling her beneath the water. It turned swiftly and attacked a second time, biting her left arm off at the shoulder and lacerating her breast. A crowd of more than two thousand people on the beach heard her screams and watched as the water reddened with blood. Paul Brokensha rushed in, grabbed the shark's tail and tried to pull it away from the girl. Effortlessly the beast flicked him away. Undaunted, the courageous man returned. With one hand he pulled at the girl and with the other he punched the shark. His actions succeeded in driving the shark away. Had it not been for this brave act the shark would undoubtedly have killed Julia outright.

The badly injured girl was carried to the beach where her bleeding wounds were tended. Now unconscious, Julia was rushed to Port Shepstone Hospital, which was unprepared for an injury of this nature. The blood bank had no stocks available for immediate transfusions so the nurses and had to be bled throughout the night. A six-hour operation repaired her injuries and ensured her recovery.

Margate's mayor immediately banned all bathing in the sea. At the following Council meeting a resolution was passed which promised payment of sixpence a pound weight for all sharks caught off Margate. As the hysteria increased the South African Navy minesweeper, *Pretoria*, was commissioned to drop depth charges and use hand grenades in the shallow water off South Coast beaches in an attempt to kill sharks.

This was the prelude to the fifth attack, which took place at Scottburgh ten days later on January 9, 1958. The victim, forty-two-year-old Deryck Prinsloo, was standing 10 meters from shore in thigh-deep water. Discolored river water flossed into the sea next to the bathing area and was churned by round surf. Because of the recent attacks tourists were reluctant to venture far into the sea. On this particular day, even though there were many people on the beach, only about twenty bathers were actually in the surf.

From out of the murky depths a shark appeared and, rushing at Prinsloo, tore at his buttocks, throwing him out of the water. It wheeled and in its second attack removed a large portion of his left thigh, almost severing the leg. It turned for the last time and ripped another portion from his buttocks and right thigh.

As lifesavers ran into the water hundreds of people gathered at the water's edge to watch the uneven battle. It is probable that the lifesavers scared the shark, which disappeared suddenly. With blood pumping from his severed femoral artery, Prinsloo was carried to shore. A tourniquet was hastily tied around his thigh and towels were used to pack the other wounds. Unconscious, he was bundled into a car and rushed to Renishaw Hospital a few kilometers away. Prinsloo was dead on arrival.

When news of this attack was announced people began leaving their hotels, no longer prepared to risk their lives in the sea. This had a snowball effect and before long thousands of tourists departed in a mass migration, leaving hotels vacant for the remainder of the holiday season.

Immediate introduction of a shark protection system now became imperative. Local authorities investigated the possibility of erecting barriers to enclose their bathing areas. Work soon began and unsightly structures appeared in the surf zones of the larger resorts.

Within a few weeks it became apparent that it was impossible to maintain these barriers because powerful waves uprooted pylons and the chicken net wire used to mesh the grids began to rust. It was realized that the cost of barrier maintenance was prohibitive but with the April school holidays drawing nearer it was essential that the beaches be protected.

An advertising campaign was undertaken by hotels and resort areas, using these shark barriers as a draw card. As a result, when the Easter holidays dawned, thousands of tourists came to the coast in what was then a record season. The nets themselves proved to be a great attraction and soon lifesavers had the arduous task of preventing bathers from hanging onto the rusting nets and breaking holes in them.

To concerned hotel owners and members of local authorities everything appeared to be under control as hundreds of people crowded into bathing enclosures. Hotels, filled to capacity, promised to make up their Christmas losses. A festive atmosphere prevailed during these days but it was to prove short-lived. At 1400 on April 3, 1958, a shark tore a man apart in the unprotected bathing area of Port Edward.

Wearing a diving mask and swim fins Nicholas François Badenhorst, a twenty-nine-year-old tourist, was swimming with his brother and a friend. In chest-deep water, the trio was 20 meters beyond two hundred other bathers concentrated nearer the shore. Badenhorst was finning along the surface peering into the clear water while his two companions caught a wave and surfed shorewards.

No one saw the first strike but as Badenhorst's cries for help alerted bathers that fearful word "shark" became uppermost in most minds. Within seconds the sea was free of humanity. As the unfortunate man struggled unaided, his wife and two children watched in horror as the large shark attacked him a second time. A middle-aged black man who had witnessed the scene ran into the sea and showing enormous courage, made his way through the breakers to the floating, lifeless form. He dragged the body back to shore where the terrible mutilations were revealed to onlookers. Both the dead man's arms had been severed, his right leg removed and a large portion torn from his abdomen.

The next day an exodus of tourists began which reduced hotels to half capacity. Even at protected bathing areas the crowds were minimal while land-locked lagoons provided alternative bathing for those who wanted to complete their holidays at the coast.

Two days later low spring tides prevailed and the tide receded, leaving the shark barriers high and dry. Uvongo's local authority took the opportunity to repair surf-inflicted damages to their barrier. A small group of people gathered next to the Uvongo river mouth to watch the workmen as they ascended the net barricade.

Fay Bester, a twenty-eight-year-old mother of four children, had come to Uvongo on her first holiday since the death of her husband in a motorcycle accident eleven months previously. On the morning of April

5, 1958, she and her family joined the crowd of officials, workmen, and dozens of other people standing knee-deep in the water at the mouth of the river.

At 1100 a shark came out of a channel and rushed at Fay, knocking her into the water. It turned swiftly, clamped its jaws around her middle and, shaking her viciously, wheeled her out of the water. As peopled vacated the river mouth their shouting and splashing drove the attacker away. The entire incident lasted only a few moments but the shark had almost bitten the woman in half, killing her instantly and leaving four orphaned children.

Midday news broadcasts announced details of the incident to a nation grown sensitive to shark attack. During the next twenty-four hour period following these broadcasts, the mass hysteria which mounted and spread through the resorts has not been equaled since. Thousands of cars streamed away from the resorts, blocking roads for kilometers at the single-carriage bridges characterizing the South Coast at the time. Hoteliers could not believe what was happening as the little resorts became virtual ghost towns within hours. South Coast residents were directly affected and during the ensuing months many hotels went bankrupt.

Few people realize how serious a shark attack can be for the economy of a resort area. Without doubt the "Black December" of 1957 is the best example of how a spate of attacks can cripple a tourist industry. It was evident that mechanical barriers were not the answer. In these early years nothing was known of what shark protection devices were available to protect bathers. Scientists launched a full-scale program to determine what counter-measures should be taken.

SHARKS AND SURVIVAL

Perry W. Gilbert

During the countless air missions flown by Allied pilots over South Pacific seas during World War II, hundreds of aircraft ended up in the ocean. Those who survived the crash or "water landing"—and many did not— were often wounded and became ready targets for shark attacks. The following firsthand accounts paint a picture of the danger faced by airmen, many of whom never made it out of the water to author their own stories.

From earliest times, vivid descriptions of encounters with sharks have been published. Many of these have been passed off as sea stories, and justly so. Nevertheless, it is true that after ship sinkings, survivors were often exposed to the attacks of these sea beasts. The evidence may be found in maritime as well as naval records of ship losses during the First and Second World Wars. Personal encounters between lone survivors and sharks have occurred at various times but most frequently during World War II when aircraft crews were forced to abandon their planes over the open sea. Information on this type of encounter comes largely from files of the Air Search and Rescue Agency. Since the end of hostilities, the occasional loss of transport and passenger aircraft over warm waters has given additional records of attacks on the open sea.

Surviving airmen were exposed to the danger of sharks under two situations. In bailouts, some spent several hours in the water buoyed up by their inflatable life preservers, before they succeeded in inflating their life rafts. Many others either lost their rafts or were unable to use them, for one reason or another. Those who were successful were forced to sit on these small pneumatic platforms, separated from the sea by a resilient deck about one-eighth inch thick which constantly took in water over the low freeboard. In either situation, the presence of sharks was a constant menace, and, while men on life rafts were somewhat better off, there was a continual anxiety that the raft might capsize. Thus, the constant proximity of one or more sharks added to the strain and indirectly drove some men to irrational acts.

According to most of the narratives reviewed, the survivors had time to reach the safety of the rafts before sharks appeared. In eleven of the thirty-eight accounts reporting the presence of sharks, the sharks appeared within thirty minutes after the men had entered the water. In thirty-six accounts, the sharks appeared during the first twenty-four hours. In some accounts of long duration in tropical waters, men reported their first, and sometimes only, shark on the fourth, ninth, or even thirteenth day.

Sharks were rarely noted until they came to the surface, usually some distance from the raft, "lazily cruising around." On approaching the raft, most sharks submerged and swam underwater before reappearing on the surface. In very few instances did sharks approach the raft directly on the surface unless there was vomit or blood in the vicinity of the raft. In these instances, survivors remarked that the sharks appeared excited and "made passes at the raft."

> About 1000 I saw a large fin . . . come toward the life raft along the streak of the dye marker. It disappeared some distance away . . . shortly afterward reappeared . . . and swam directly toward the raft, approaching quite close, it submerged and swam directly under the raft . . . it was about 12 feet long. It rolled over and reappeared on the other side . . . we all sat very quiet, stopped bailing out the bloody vomit, and the radar man abandoned the idea of defecating over the side for fear of capsizing. The shark repeated this behavior several times at varied intervals but at no time seemed concerned with us or touched the raft.

In another case, this one off Japan in June, after the survivors had been vomiting into the water for about half an hour, eight sharks made passes at the raft as if to upset it. Although the men fired some thirty rounds of .38 caliber at them, it was another one-and-one-half hours before the sharks left.

Sharks sometimes remained under the raft day and night and often bumped against the raft bottom. Off Iwo Jima in early summer:

> The raft was followed a great part of the time (ten days) by sharks . . . frequently close enough to cause fear of upset . . . On two occasions . . . shot a shark from above . . . each time, the shark sounded and did not bother us again. These fish came close enough so that they could almost be touched. Aside from the nuisance, they did not bother the raft.

The mere presence of sharks close by can be unnerving. They exerted enough force against the raft deck at times to lift the occupant 3 or 5 inches into the air; this was painful to those whose buttocks ached from raft drumming and made sleep impossible.

One seventeen-day group of survivors stated that sharks never left them and became increasingly bolder, leaping out of the water and spraying the occupants, or battering the soft deck with their tails while trying to stun the fish under the raft:

> Late in the afternoon a shark about 4 feet long struck at the raft and going right over my shoulder slid into the raft. It took a bite out of C. One of the men and myself caught the shark by the tail and pulled him out of the raft. C. became delirious and died about four hours later . . .

Survivors in Carley floats were more liable to attack, since the open mesh of these rafts offered no protection to the dangling limbs.

Sharks often follow floating objects because the smaller fish on which they feed take refuge in the shadows. Several survivors commented that the sharks' interest in the raft was not for its occupants but for the fish that clustered beneath it:

> I believe that it was feeding on the small fish in the shade of the raft. There might have been more than one shark. After the animal demonstrated its benign attitude toward us, our chief concern was that it would abrade our boat with its hide and deflate it, or that it would accidentally capsize us . . . Its approach was

heralded by panicked flights of flying fish . . . It was always chasing fish out into the open and feeding on them.

An F4U pilot who spent nine days in a raft drifting from Rabaul to Bougainville wrote:

> From practically the first day, sharks were continually hitting up against the boat trying to get the small fish under it. I was quite scared at first, but soon got accustomed to it when I learned what they were after.

Recognition of this aspect of shark behavior gave the man in the raft some comfort and helped make the situation bearable, borne out by such remarks as "Sharks around all the time—no bother," and "He never came very close and did not constitute a problem." But though men sometimes achieved a sense of confidence toward sharks, situations developed which sorely tried their faith:

> He never came very close and did not constitute a problem until two unidentified planes appeared on the horizon at 1,000 feet and coming toward us. We were just debating which was worse, sharks or a strafing by Japs, when they veered off. A few hours later a submarine appeared, and again we debated whether to go overside with the shark or sweat it out in the raft.
>
> Half a dozen sharks were with me day and night. Only one, however, made an attempt to attack, and it was a small one about 4 feet long. Most of them that I saw were at least 6 or 7 feet in length. My lone would-be attacker rolled over on its side and turned almost belly up to get into position to bite.
>
> I could see its curved mouth, ugly teeth, and beady, pig-like eyes . . . fortunately, he failed to carry out his attack.

Although a few men became accustomed to sharks around their raft, all raft occupants regarded them at least with suspicion, if not with fear, and tried in one way or another to drive them away. All expressed relief at their departure.

Although most men remained quiet when a large shark cruised nearby, hoping they would not be noticed, some tried to drive away smaller sharks circling around them by spanking the water with their paddles. In several of these instances the sharks were attracted to the paddles and tried to bite them. The interrogators usually interpreted this reaction as one of attack, but few of these incidents can be regarded as unprovoked or deliberate attacks.

Unproved attacks by sharks on boats are a matter of record. Coppleson (1958 and 1962) cites instances of sharks tearing off large pieces of wood. Fortunately, this type of encounter was not known to sea survivors, or the presence of sharks around their life rafts would have given them far more concern. The record provides only one incident of an attack on a life raft in which the occupant just managed to survive. It is not likely that this was a unique incident; probably others under similar attack did not fare as well.

The incident took place in St. George's Channel between New Britain and New Ireland during the Rabaul strikes and involved a lone Navy fighter pilot who spent eight days in his dinghy before being rescued off Cape St. George. The pilot was able to inflate and crawl into his raft a few minutes after "ditching." He vaguely remembered something striking his foot while he was in the water. He then noticed he had lost the heel and part of the back of his left shoe and, from the scratches on the shoe, hazarded a guess that a shark had bitten it off, though he saw no sharks at all until sundown of his third day when:

> There was a constant cloud of minnows following the boat at all times. I believe they fed on the minute marine life that collected on its bottom, sides, etc. That night larger fish came to feed on those minnows, then larger ones to get them; finally, the boys with their peculiar dorsal fins arrived to see what the fuss was about. There were three of them that I could see.
>
> Finally one of them flashed directly under the boat, hitting it with his back. He then turned and started striking it with his head. About the third time he came up to the boat slowly right

on the surface and I shot him through the head from point-blank range. He thrashed for nearly a minute, then I could see him sinking down. The others did not touch him. One other shark still stayed about 10 feet away and I fired at his fin scaring him off. After it became dark I had no more trouble.

That night [his fifth] I shot another shark and tried to bring him aboard, as I'd heard their liver, heart, etc., were good, but he was too slimy and still thrashing around slightly so I gave up. I also found that their hide was like 00 sandpaper!

[At sundown on his sixth night] The usual ruckus of feeding fish started around the boat and shortly afterwards the sharks arrived. After swimming directly under the boat several times and hitting it with his back and fin, one large one about seven feet (formerly the sharks had averaged about 4 to 5 feet) came to the surface and started to bump the boat with his nose.

This had become a rather commonplace procedure with me by this time and I put the .45 about 6 inches from his head and was about to give him his iron for the day. The gun would not fire as the slide had rusted and wasn't all the way forward. Frantically I tried to push it home as the shark unmolested started banging my boat in earnest. Finally, in my excitement, I ejected the shell and it landed in the bottom of the boat and cleverly concealed itself under some other gear there. By now the shark was going berserk (evidently smelling me) and coming up underneath the boat and knocking us both completely out of the water. It then came to the surface again and made rushes at me, spinning the boat completely around 360 degrees several times.

During all this I was holding grimly on and although I have no recollection of it, undoubtedly screaming! He came to the surface again, lay on his back and began snapping at the boat. Never was I so grateful to Mother Nature for the placement of his mouth. I'd given up trying to load the .45 and was swinging it by the muzzle at him. I smashed him in the eye, on "his very vulnerable nose," and his "soft" belly. He turned over then and I started to pound him on the top of his head. He was as hard as steel there, and I later discovered I'd partly flattened the little steel eyelet on the butt of the gun where the lanyard is attached. He rolled over again still snapping at the boat and I remembered a capsule of chlorine I had so I tried to get it out of my pocket, with no success. I had dropped the gun and was searching my pockets with one hand and was hitting my voracious friend with my other fist. In that ill-advised action, I got two fair-sized splits in my forefinger, when one of his snaps and one of my blows became beautifully timed.

Giving up the chlorine idea I seized the dye marker can and dumped some of it on his face, and the action ceased. The whole action had lasted from five to ten minutes. Whether the shark realized I was in the boat or whether he was merely venting his rage on this strange yellow object I will never know, but he made a savage and sustained attack and the ultimate end would have been the same, mine!

After his departure I took stock of the situation and was depressed beyond all hope. The bottom of my boat had eighteen holes in it. One was a slit about 4 inches long, another a round hole about the size of my fist. The rest were assorted shapes and sizes, all smaller. This was not so bad, but at the small end of the boat in the inflated part there were five slits all leaking badly. I must confess I gave up and believing I was doomed, drank all my remaining water thinking that at least I didn't need to be thirsty any longer.

[The seventh evening] My gun worked OK and I killed or badly wounded two sharks and had no further trouble . . .

After my first encounter with sharks, I never even considered going over the side of the boat to avoid strafing . . . After the skirmishes with the sharks I'd have about five or ten small minnows in my boat and tried eating them. I thought they were better than the pemmican.

It would appear that swimmers deprived of life rafts held little hope for life when sharks were attracted to them. But the example of Arias (1941) is not unique; there are other instances of swimmers untouched, even though attended by one or more sharks. The following case histories serve to reveal the nature of these situations:

A Navy pilot who ditched off Kikai-Shima in the northern Ryukyus entered the water fully dressed except for his shoes and was supported by a Mae West for the one and one-quarter hours he remained in the water before rescue:

> Fifteen minutes after landing, W. discovered a shark about 6 feet long, 5 to 6 feet below the water and directly under him. The shark made no runs at him and W. took no affirmative action except to swim easily which was all that was necessary in order stay up in the water . . . A second shark about 10 to 12 feet long was not noted until the last twenty minutes before pickup. It might have been around during the whole period but W. did not see it until it was about 5 feet away and after it had come to the surface when the dorsal fin and tail projected above the water. At this time he used dye to indicate his position to the approaching plane, and while holding in the dye, the second shark swam through the discolored area with no indication that it saw W.

At least four sharks came within 25 yards of another pilot swimming ashore in the Southwest Pacific, and not one of them made a determined attack. The amount of clothing he wore is not mentioned in his story:

> I left the raft at 1000 because I could see the shore . . . after a two-hour swim I seemed to be a little closer . . . a few minutes later while swimming on my back I looked to my left and about 3 feet away I saw a shark's fin and he was swimming along beside me. He then turned into me so I rolled over quickly and pushed him away with my right arm. He went out in front of me a few yards and did a 180-degree turn and came back under my stom-

ach. I thrashed the water with arms and legs and I think I scared him away . . . About two hours later there were two of them about 25 yards behind me, and seemed to be following me. After another hour of swimming I saw a splash and a shark's fin in front of me about 10 yards to my left . . . I began to realize it was a swim for my life, so made up my mind not to get panicky but to keep plugging along until I got there, or the sharks got me.

A Navy ensign who parachuted into Philippine waters off Cape Engano during the carrier strike in October 1944 was just as lucky:

D. hit the water on his back. He received quite a jolt but was able to untangle himself and get out of his shoes and backpack. He found his life raft had shaken off when his parachute opened. The front half of his life jacket had a rip in it and the back half had to be inflated orally every half hour . . . As he swam his socks gradually worked off, leaving his feet as a lure for sharks . . . which promptly put in an appearance. He was shadowed by about four sharks, 4 to 5 feet in length. They did not bother him as long as he continued to kick. As soon as he stopped to rest, one of them would make a pass at him. All of these were dry runs except one in which the shark grazed his legs and left tooth marks. He was picked up by a destroyer after eight hours in the water.

During a forty-two-hour survival in the Pacific, eight of the twelve men who survived the ditching were fully clothed, although some removed or lost their shoes after entering the water. They held themselves up with a salvaged wing float and a sleeping bag and lashed themselves together. Later, they found a package of emergency food, a blanket, and a thermos half-filled with water. One of the survivors was located by the firing of his .45 automatic, and, as he swam towards the group, his companions cautiously watched his approach for fear that he was out of his mind and might shoot them. One man died, and his life vest was taken by another who had none. About this time, sharks appeared and the men tried to drive them away by shooting and kicking. Although they were not bothered particularly by sharks during the darkness, they continued kicking. At daybreak, one man was bitten slightly, became frightened, and died during the second night. Two others became delirious and had to be protected because they made no effort to help themselves. At 0500 of the third morning, the remaining six men were rescued by a passing merchant vessel. The rescuers were greatly agitated by the presence of sharks among the survivors, one of whom noted it and remarked, "We got a kick out of it."

Timing in rescue was all that saved a few survivors, wounded by repeated rushes of one or more aroused sharks. Two documented incidents show that even under such desperate circumstances one should not give up all hope. The first is the case of Lt. Comdr. Kabat (1944), who floated at night without clothing or shoes in a kapok life jacket off Guadalcanal. At dawn he felt a scratching, tickling sensation in his left foot:

> Slightly startled, I . . . held it up. It was gushing blood . . . I peered into the water . . . not 10 feet away was the glistening, brown back of a great fish . . . swimming away. The real fear did not hit me until I saw him turn and head back toward me. He didn't rush . . . but breaking the surface of the water came in a steady direct line. I kicked and splashed tremendously, and this time he veered off me . . . went off about 20 feet and swam back and forth. Then he turned . . . and came from the same angle toward my left . . . When he was almost upon me I thrashed out . . . brought my fist down on his nose . . . again and again. He was thrust down about 2 feet . . . swam off and waited. I discovered that he had torn off of a piece of my left hand. Then . . . again at the same angle to my left . . . I managed to hit him on the eyes, the nose. The flesh was torn from my left arm . . . At intervals of ten or fifteen minutes he would ease off from his slow swimming and bear directly toward me, coming in at my left. Only twice did he go beneath me. Helpless against this type of attack I feared it most but because I was so nearly flat on top of the water, he

seemed unable to get at me from below . . . The bit toe on my left foot was dangling. A piece of my right heel was gone. My left elbow, hand, and calf were torn. If he did not actually sink his teeth into me, his rough hide would scrape great pieces off my skin. The salt water stanched the flow of blood somewhat and I was not conscious of great pain. [In the excitement of trying to attract the attention of a ship going by, the officer forgot the shark, which struck again and bit into his thigh, exposing the bone. At this point he was seen, and several sailors with rifles on the ship began firing at the shark.] A terrible fear of being shot to death in the water when rescue was so near swept over me. I screamed and pleaded and cried for them to stop. The shark was too close. They would hit me first.

The second case involved two Navy aviators, Almond and Reading, who ditched in the central Pacific, 68 miles east of Wallis Island. Reading was knocked unconscious by the impact, but his radioman, Almond, managed to lift him from the cockpit and put on and inflate his life jacket for him before the plane sank. Here are the significant parts of Lieutenant Reading's report:

After I came to, A. told me the plane had sunk in two minutes and that he didn't have time to salvage the life raft. He pulled both our "dye markers" and had a parachute alongside of him. He did not have any pants on at all except for shorts . . . We soon lost the chute and began drifting away from the dye. It was within a very short time (about 1/2 hour) when sharks were quite apparent swimming around us. A. and I were tied together by dye marker cords and it made it difficult to make any headway. An hour later we heard aircraft and I said to A., "Let's kick and splash around to see if we can't attract their attention." It failed, but suddenly A. said he felt something strike his right foot and that it hurt. I told him to get on my back and keep his right foot out of the water, but before he could, the sharks struck again and we were both jerked under water for a second. I knew that we were in for it as there were more than five sharks around and blood all around us. He showed me his leg and not only did he have bites all over his right leg, but his left thigh was badly mauled. He wasn't in any particular pain except every time they struck I knew it and felt the jerk. I finally grabbed my binoculars and started swinging them at the passing sharks. It was a matter of seconds when they struck again. We both went under and this time I found myself separated from A. I also was the recipient of a wallop across the cheek bone by one of the flaying tails of a shark. From that moment on I watched A. bob about from the attacks. His head was under water and his body jerked as the sharks struck it. As I drifted away . . . sharks continually swam about and every now and then I could feel one with my foot. At midnight I sighted a YP [yard patrol] boat and was rescued after calling for help.

Jaws of Death

Xavier Maniguet

Leave it to a few accounts in plain language to drive home the visceral crux of a shark attack, well demonstrated by these anecdotes from "The Jaws of Death," an anthology that, a decade ago, caused a national stir in France.

When, in 1950, a transport aircraft linking Puerto Rico and Miami ditched in the sea off Florida, many passengers survived, floating in their life jackets. Shortly afterwards, the pilot of a plane that flew over them signaled that a number of them were being attacked by a horde of sharks. Each tragedy was made obvious to him by the red patches that appeared on the orange specks of the lifejackets. Another spotter-plane pilot was likewise traumatized by the spectacle that presented itself in 1987 in the Caribbean. At the beginning of October that year, in a clandestine operation, 168 Dominicans left their country for the United States, via Puerto Rico. Aboard the boat were women, children, old people, and men packed in together. For some unknown reason the boat capsized. All the passengers found themselves in the water in a warm tropical sea, which should allow for relatively long survival. The castaways being only 8 kilometers from the coast, they undertook to swim toward it. Their efforts were to last twelve hours, in the course of which they had to face the blazing sun, a current running against them, and, above all, uncompromising aggressors, the sharks attracted by their injuries.

Head of the civil defense, Eugenio Cabral, flew over the spot in a helicopter and looked on, powerless, at a horrifying spectacle. "The sharks seemed to have gone mad," he explained. "At first they were devouring only the corpses, but very quickly they attacked all over the place. They were big sharks, makos and hammerheads, and the water had turned red." Of the 168 passengers, only eight survivors were rescued!

It is obvious that these poor wretches were victims of that aspect of shark behavior which is not regular but is incredibly dangerous: the feeding frenzy. Knowing the uncontrollable murderous excitation that seizes sharks at such times, and the terrible vulnerability of a man in the sea, it is easy to understand how only a minute minority escaped the massacre.

Still on the subject of wrecks in tropical waters, Christian Troebst reports the case of a relatively lucky victim.

"During the war an American pilot fell into the sea with two other airmen just off the South American coast. At the end of five hours one of the latter died of exhaustion, and the pilot started to swim pushing the body in front of him. Suddenly, something seized and shook the body, which then disappeared for good beneath the water. The survivors continued to swim through the night, but, after a few hours, the second airman also died. The pilot again started to push ahead of him. Meanwhile the moon had risen, and the brightness suddenly enabled him to distinguish the dorsal fins of a large number of sharks swimming in a circle around him. Once more a jolt shook the corpse, which briefly sank under the water and then rose again to the surface, now without feet. Horrified, the swimmer turned it and grabbed it by the shoulders. The body immediately submerged a second time, only to reappear and resubmerge. The sharks devoured it little by little up to the shoulders. At dawn they began to attack the pilot. The latter knew he was very close to the shore, and yelling and beating the water frenetically, he made it to land unharmed."

An American soldier whose destroyer was sunk off Guadalcanal reported: "I had been drifting for eleven hours when I suddenly felt my left foot itching. I lifted it above the water: it was dripping with blood. I immersed my head and I saw the shark charging at me. I shook my arms and legs violently and it passed very close, brushing against me. It turned about on itself and came back straight at me. I clenched my fist and delivered it a blow on the jaw, with all my might. It moved away but not without having torn off a piece of my left hand; it attacked again and, once more, I hammered it in the eyes and the nose. When it moved off, I discovered that it had slashed my left arm. My heel had disappeared, too. At this point a lifeboat approached. I frantically beckoned it and forgot the shark. It tore away a piece of my hip, exposing the bone. Then I was hoisted into the boat."

Just before Christmas 1948, Tony Latona, a thirteen-year-old boy, was recovered on a beach in Cuba. He was in critical condition and around his waist was wearing a life buoy in a sorry state. He had just spent forty hours in the water, and his story was difficult to believe at first. He told how he had been playing with another boy, fourteen-year-old Bent Jeppsen, on the after deck of the Danish ship *Grete Maersk* when Jeppsen went overboard about 14 kilometers from Cape Maisi in Cuba. Tony threw Jeppsen a life buoy, then jumped overboard himself to help him. Their shouts of course were not heard and the ship disappeared. They had been in the water for two hours when they saw sharks arriving to attack them. One of them attacked Jeppsen and left two deep gashes in his left foot. Latona's story went on: "We banged and banged until the sharks moved away. I told Jeppsen that the blood in the water would send the sharks crazy. I told him to take off his trousers and tie them around his foot to help stop the bleeding. We did not see the sharks any more, but they can't have been very far away because an hour later, when Jeppsen's trousers went, the sharks were back upon us within a few minutes. They passed just behind me and tried to grab Jeppsen. We continued to keep them at a distance, but they came back every quarter of an hour. And then a shark caught him again by the same foot. He complained about pain. The sharks came back more often taking less and less notice of our efforts to keep them off. Soon enough another one bit Jeppsen under the arm. He wept when the shark tore away his flesh. Another one arrived which snatched away his knee. He howled and began to slip down. He sank beneath the water screaming "My foot!" He emerged again, screaming and fighting, and then he vanished again. That was the last time I saw him. I saw some blood in the water, so I sat in the life buoy and I kept my feet on the edges, above the water, paddling with my hands until I was too tired. When day broke I was near the coast but the daytime currents pushed me back out to sea. The following night the sharks returned, one of them removing the bottom of my trousers. On the morning of the second day, a current finally brought me ashore." Again we notice in this example the very selective attraction of the shark to the prey that is bleeding, maintaining a total indifference to any other potential prey, even very close by. This behavior is very different from the feeding frenzy, in the course of which any object inert or living is indiscriminately torn up and swallowed.

Commander Kabat also found out to his cost how relentlessly a shark can pursue its prey when his destroyer, the *Duncan*, sank off Guadalcanal in 1942 and he found himself in the water for a whole night with an old kapok life jacket and two small empty powder kegs as his only means of keeping afloat. Shortly after dusk he felt an itching in the region of his left foot and discovered that it was bleeding. He then noticed the brownish shadow of a shark less than three meters from him. The shark swam around him several times and then attacked again. Kabat tried to hold it off by punching it. After the animal had left, he found that a piece of flesh had been removed from his left hand. At intervals of about fifteen minutes he was attacked and wounded—a little more each time. At first his big toe was removed, then a piece of his right hip, then another from his left shoulder, from his right hand, from his buttocks. Kabat noted: "When it was not planting its teeth in my flesh, its rasping hide was removing great lumps of skin." In the course of the attacks which followed, his thigh was sliced into so deeply that the femur was visible.

Statistical study of attacks on people in the sea tends to prove that the risk is greater if the victim is not clothed. During the Second World War, the engine of a reconnaissance plane broke down 110 kilometers east of the Wallis Islands and 400 kilometers west of Western Samoa in the open Pacific. Lieutenant Reading managed to put down his craft without too much damage but he was knocked senseless by the impact. It was his radio operator Ahmond who managed to get him out of the cockpit and to release his life jacket before the plane sank. On contact with the water it was not long before Reading regained consciousness, and the two men lost in the open ocean opened their fluorescein bags in the hope of being picked up before night came. They tethered themselves to each other using the strings of their life jackets, and they waited. Reading was clothed and Ahmond was wearing shorts.

After about half an hour the sharks made their appearance. Shortly afterwards, Ahmond signaled that something had knocked against his right foot. His foot was bleeding and he tried to keep it out of the water. The sharks came back and the two men were dragged beneath the surface for a moment. The water around them was reddened by the blood and there were now five sharks harassing them. Not only did Ahmond's right leg bear several wounds, but his left thigh was deeply gashed as well. He felt no pain even though the sharks continued to harass him. Reading struck those which passed within his reach with his binoculars, but almost at once the beasts returned to attack Ahmond. The two men disappeared underwater again, and, when they resurfaced, Reading discovered that he was separated from his comrade. It was then that he was half knocked out by a flick of a tail on his chin, but the shark responsible for the blow was still only interested in Ahmond, who was now completely underwater and neither he nor his life jacket emerged again. The monsters continued circling around and from time to time Reading could feel them brushing his feet, but he was still not attacked. He was rescued after sixteen hours in the water, sixteen hours of terrible anguish surrounded by sharks and by the remains of the man who had saved his life.

It is not only being clothed that can reduce the risk of being attacked. When there are several people in the water it is also essential to group together back to back. Being in a coherent group enables heat loss to be reduced appreciably and, in tropical waters, a look out can be kept for sharks, this also permitting one to shield oneself against attack without worrying about what is going on behind one's back. It is also possible that the combined bulk of several people in the water joined together in a "pack" will, by its very nature, arouse the shark's distrust as much as its curiosity.

Dr. Llano reports that the longest period of survival of men in the sea in shark-infested waters involved a group of soldiers who spent forty-two hours shoulder to shoulder in the water. Of the twelve who survived without being attacked, eight were fully clothed, even though some of them removed or lost their shoes.

• • •

In 1942, the *Dorsetshire* was sunk by mines in the middle of the Indian Ocean. Commander Agar very quickly realized that, for the hundreds of men around him in the sea, the danger came above all from sharks. He ordered his men to gather together all the dead bodies floating around them, so all the survivors positioned themselves backs facing inwards around the macabre "platform." They remained like this in the open sea for thirty-six hours, battling against the sharks which gathered around the sixty corpses. The sharks were able to divert their aggression on to the dead men, sparing the survivors who seemed to be less easy prey.

Vic Beaver was a seventy-four-year-old Australian who held a number of national game-fishing records. On March 11, 1977, he set off aboard his boat in Brisbane Bay accompanied by two friends who liked to share his favorite pastime. It was well into the night when one of these, Harrison, discerned through the rain the lights of a cargo vessel on a collision course toward them. When the 2500-ton ship rammed their boat, they sank immediately and found themselves in the sea, their only means of buoyancy a 1-meter ice container and an air bed. The three men were to cling to the container as best they could for thirty-six hours. Small sharks came and threatened them, and then a big one joined them. When this shark attacked Vic Beaver, Harrison tried hard to hold on to Vic and to deter his aggressor by kicking and punching it but to no avail. Later he recounted: "I tried to keep Vic with me but he was being pulled out of the container. Vic simply said to me: 'It's got me again. So long, friends, that's how it goes.' And then he vanished. That's all he said when the shark took him. John and I tried to huddle together inside the ice box, but we could only protect our heads and our shoulders and the shark was still beneath us. I punched and kicked it and cut myself slightly. The shark then began to circle us again and John cried out: 'It's had my foot!' He told me to stay in the box, and then the shark dragged him under the water. I tried to climb up the box for safety, but the bastard tried to climb with me."

An hour after this second fatal attack, Harrison was rescued by the crew of another fishing boat. The shark must have been either a Great White or a Tiger, as both species live in the bay.

● ● ●

Coppleson reports another drama that occurred unexpectedly, again in Australia, in North Queensland. Ray Boundy was skipper of a 14 meter fishing boat trawling near the Townsville reefs. One of the trawl's hoists happened to break, throwing it off balance, and then a huge wave overturned the boat. Boundy took refuge on the keel along with his crewmate Denis Murphy, aged twenty-four, and Linda Horton, aged twenty-one. They decided to leave the sinking wreck, taking with them a surfboard, a life buoy, and some pieces of polystyrene, and to try and reach the nearby reefs where they could be spotted.

At dawn on July 25, 1983, they were no more than 8 kilometers from the town of Lodestone, but nobody saw them, not even the aircraft that passed above them in its searches. Shortly after nightfall, a shark appeared and began to push at the board, the pieces of foam, the life buoy and the three castaways. "We didn't take too much notice of this," Boundy recounted, "thinking that if we didn't annoy it, it would leave us alone." The shark at first took an interest in Boundy's leg, but he kicked it with his other foot and the animal disappeared.

Ten minutes later, a big wave knocked the three castaways into the sea and the shark immediately returned. Murphy began to yell: "It's had my leg, the bastard's had my leg!" and then, a few seconds later: "This time, that's it; you and Lindy, go, get away," and he swam three or four breast strokes toward the shark. In the darkness Boundy and Lindy heard curses together with pounding in the water testifying to a desperate struggle between man and animal. They saw their companion's body emerge face down, and then disappear into the shark's mouth.

Everything went quiet for the next two hours, and then the monster came back to circle them from 4:00 A.M. onwards. Boundy continues: "Lindy was sitting in the snaffle of the life buoy with her feet out of the water resting on a sheet of foam. I was practically sure that it was the same shark that came back. This time it approached slowly, then suddenly seized Lindy, its enormous jaws around her arms and her chest while she was still seated in the buoy, shaking her three or four times. She let out only a small cry just as the shark crushed her rib cage, and I knew almost instantaneously that she was dead."

Boundy used two pieces of foam by way of paddles in an attempt to get away, but just after sunrise the shark reappeared again, to circle around him: "I thought I would never escape, for it was circling nearer and nearer to me, and then I caught sight of a reef protruding above the surface." Boundy succeeded in surfing as far as the reef by making use of a piece of foam. There a plane spotted him and a helicopter of the RAAF picked him up. The attacker or attackers were probably Tiger Sharks or large Whaler Sharks (*Carcharhinus obscurus*), very widespread in this zone.

FIRST ENCOUNTERS

Marty Snyderman

"Somehow as a kid I knew that sharks were not the beasts that so many people claimed they were," writes author and filmmaker Marty Snyderman. In this short personal account, Snyderman runs down an event that spawned his telling words, an event in which the "beasts" were more clearly on the boat than in the water.

The boat was alive with activity. The crew was hustling to help one fisherman after another land his prizes. We had been into the fish all morning, but the last ten or fifteen minutes were the best I had ever seen. I hadn't done a lot of deep-sea fishing in my life, but I was savvy enough to know that we were in the middle of a big hit, and that is why a lot of people fish. Big groupers and red snappers were being hauled in over the side at a clip, faster than I could count. Somewhat in the middle of the melee, I got my first double ever, two fish at one time on a single line. My snappers probably weren't the biggest on the boat, but my smile was. At the age of nine, I was out on my own, fishing on a sport charter out of Panama City, Florida.

Neither of my parents was a serious fisher, though Dad had taken me fishing often enough for me to be competent. But it was really my Uncle Herb who exposed me to the outdoors. Without his guidance I probably never would have found myself out here in the middle of nowhere some 60 miles (95 kilometers) offshore with a boatload of men and women who seemed to think that fishing is what life is all about. My family was on vacation and, as a special treat, my mom and dad have given me a day of deep-sea fishing. No one else in my family wanted to go, so I went by myself. To my mind, I was in great company.

The calendar might have said August, but it was Christmas morning as far as I was concerned. When my folks had taken me down to the dock and put me on the boat the previous evening, they were obviously worried that I would get seasick and be a pain in the neck to everyone on the boat. But for some reason the crew and a number of the fishermen had taken an interest in me. I had stood back and watched a group of beer-drinking, cigar-smoking, big-talking fishermen play poker and swap lies for as long as I could keep my eyes open as we headed out of port. These guys seemed like real men to me.

The next morning I was up bright and early, probably three or four hours earlier than normal, but I just didn't want to miss anything. I watched the loudest talkers at the poker table set up their rods and reels, and bait their hooks. I tried to imitate their every move. Somehow I had managed to catch a couple of decent fish early in the morning, and I was beginning to feel like I was one of the gang. All I lacked was a beer, a cigar, and some understanding of the terms "full house," "straight," "High Chicago," and a couple of others I knew not to repeat around Mom and Dad when I got back to shore.

About midday we got into a big school of actively feeding bottom-fish. I had never seen so many fish being caught at one time. I watched one man get his line tangled with another man's, and I added a few new works to my quickly expanding vocabulary. I vowed not to be as clumsy as the fellow who had caused the tangle during the best fishing of the day.

I was fishing near the stern, and suddenly I head a deep voice toward the bow hollering out "We got a beast up here. Everybody in." I didn't know what "Everybody in" meant, but I knew I needed to pay some attention. Somebody was serious about something. Then they all started reeling in their lines and putting their rods away. I did the same as I asked the fisherman everyone called "Hook Up" what was going on. I remember him looking down at me and saying, "We got a beast, Kiddo. Somebody has hooked up with a big shark."

A shark! God almighty, it really was Christmas in August. I couldn't wait to see what the beast would look like. I reeled in my line as fast as I could, put my rod away, and ran to the bow. It was elbow to elbow, but I ducked down and wriggled in between the fishermen and made my way to the rail. I couldn't see anything in the water, but the man everyone was looking at was standing at the rail only a few feet away. His rod was bent over hard and he appeared to be doing all he could to hang on. Sweat was popping out on his forehead, and his biceps were bulging.

I heard a crew member say, "This is a shark, no doubt. Probably a bull. I suspect it's a big one." I didn't know if "bull" meant a male shark or a kind of shark, but I was soon going to find out. As the struggle between fisherman and shark continued, some of the other fishermen began to cheer their pal on. Others began to taunt him, telling him that their grandmothers could reel in faster than he could.

I heard a man standing next to me shout out "Someone ought to shoot the bastard as soon as we see him. Best way to land a shark is to plug him in the head first." He seemed to know what he was talking about, but he smelled like beer and sweat, and I didn't like him because of that. I didn't move away because I couldn't wait to see what this shark was going to look like.

I imagined some kind of teeth-chomping monster than was half the size of our boat. I expected the shark to be snapping and biting at everything in sight. I asked another fisherman what they were going to do with the shark when the man reeled it in next to the boat, and the fellow replied that the crew would kill it. He said they would shoot it if it was too big to take with a gaff. Then he told me that, depending on how big the shark was, they would cut it loose or haul it on deck.

The fight continued, and the fisherman was obviously winning as he continued to reel in the line, but he did have to fight for every inch. My anticipation heightened as the crew took up positions, peering down into the water and trying to catch the first glimpse of the shark. A few moments later, I saw it plain as day. It was a shark all right, though not nearly as big or as frightening-looking as I had imagined.

As soon as the shark came into view, someone hollered to make room for the crew. The crowd parted, and a crewman with a rifle in hand made his way to the bow rail. Several fishermen began to say things like "Plug the bastard right in the brain. Take a hell of a shot to do that, you know. They ain't nearly as smart as they are mean. Brain's about the size of a pea. Last time this s.o.b. will steal any of our fish. Only good shark is a dead shark, blast him."

All of a sudden I found myself feeling sorry for the shark. Here we were, a bunch of fishermen who had put bait in the water, trying to kill an animal that they swore was mean, stupid, and ought to be killed for eating the bait, even though it was perfectly okay to take the bait if you were a big ole red snapper or grouper. It was pretty clear to me that if anyone who killed anything that day should be punished, there were a lot of fishermen in serious trouble, myself included.

Secretly I began to hope the shark would cut the line and get free, but I heard someone say that he was "hooked good." I couldn't tell, but I feared he was right. I could feel the sense of excitement building in the fishermen. They wanted to see the shark die. I could hear it, feel it, and smell it. I wanted the shark to get away, but I knew better than to say anything.

When I looked at the shark, I saw a tired, struggling animal that was fighting for its life. I didn't see a beast or a bastard. I saw a frightened fish that was nearly exhausted. The shark wasn't trying to bite anyone or anything; it was just tugging on the line with the last of its energy. It was big, at least 8 or 10 feet (2 or 3 meters) long, but it was almost out of fight.

I couldn't understand why we had to kill the shark if we weren't going to haul it in and eat it. It seemed we were just going to kill it to satisfy some crazy inner need.

Within seconds after the shark was reeled up to the surface, the crewman unloaded a series of rifle shots into the sharks head and back. Liquid oozed out of the shark, and the animal soon quit moving. The crew decided just to cut the animal loose, and as soon as they did, most of the fishermen hurried back to their positions to get their hooks into the water. I stood at the rail and watched the lifeless form spiral down toward the depths. I felt angry and guilty. We didn't have to kill that shark. We could have cut it free. And since we did kill it, we should have done everything we could to haul it on board and use it somehow.

How, I wondered, could grown people allow such senseless killing to occur?

When the shark's body finally disappeared into the depths, I turned and looked at the other fishermen on the boat. I didn't like them any-more. I didn't know what sharks were, but I was certain they weren't what these fishermen thought they were. This shark was merely an animal living its life that paid the ultimate price for being in the wrong place at the wrong time.

A few days later I was snorkeling in front of the motel where my family was staying during our vacation, and I swam over a small sand shark. As soon as it detected my presence, it hurriedly swam away. It was obvious to me that this shark was more scared than I was.

These incidents are vividly etched in my memory. Somehow as a kid I knew that sharks were not the beasts that so many people claimed they were, and I knew that I wanted to find out what these animals were really all about.

Almost forty years later, I continue to be intrigued by sharks. In fact, I have just begun an eighteen-month-long project making a film about the natural history of sharks for the PBS series *Nature*. Clearly my first encounters with sharks made a big impression on me.

Bare Fists against a Shark

H. R. Kabat

When the new destroyer USS Duncan was torpedoed off Savo Island, deep in the South Pacific in October of 1942, Lieutenant Commander H. R. Kabat soon found himself floating in the water, relatively unharmed, but supported only by a kapok life jacket. In fact the commander's remarkable ordeal was just getting under way.

Grievously wounded, the new destroyer *Duncan* was going down. It was October 1942, and the *Duncan* as part of a force of four cruisers and five destroyers had been shooting it out in the darkness with the Tokyo Express, which was trying hard to land troops and supplies to reinforce Guadalcanal against our marines there. Only a few months earlier I had received my orders as chief engineer of the *Duncan* and here I was all of a sudden giving orders to abandon ship. Forty or fifty shells had struck us and the three officers who were senior to me had been killed or carried away. The *Duncan* was aflame and sinking, and I was in command.

Never, in my worst nightmares, could I have imagined myself in such a situation. Nor could I have imagined myself fighting off a shark alone and weaponless in the water, as I was presently to be doing.

I had to face the fact that our lifeboats were burned and that we had only two life rafts. Our other rafts had been thrown over the side some days before to survivors of a carrier when the *Duncan*, already loaded with a thousand men, had been unable to take on more.

The few of our men who were wounded were lowered to the rafts. The rest of us had our life jackets. There was a casualness about the activities. Each man took a drink of water. Many of the men searched around for mattress covers, ammunition cans or whatever else might be of use. They began to gather at the stern, stepping off into the water that was now so close. There was no panic, rather, the men had to be urged to hurry.

I waited, directing the men into the water to stay together and to swim toward the island off to port. I had no way of knowing which island this was or who held it, but from the deck I had seen its mass standing out a little darker than the night. I took off my shoes and trousers and, finding two aluminum powder cans about 5 or 6 inches in diameter and a couple of feet long, I tied these together with a piece of line, thinking that their buoyancy might help to support me in the water. I had on a kapok life jacket and carried also a rubber inflatable jacket.

The water was cool, but not cold. Towing my powder cans, I paddled clear of the ship as fast as I could. When I seemed far enough away in case she exploded, I lay back in the water, resting. I could hear the voices of the men calling back and forth to one another, but I could see no one—nothing but the blackness of the water, the *Duncan* burning steadily, and the dark mass of land several miles away. If I hoped to swim to that island, I would have to save my strength. I took out the rubber life jacket and attempted to blow it up, but it hung limp. It must have been punctured, so I threw it away.

I now began to notice the stars crowding the clear sky. The battle seemed remote and long past. The quiet and easy motion of the water began to relax some of the tautness within me. Surely the daylight would bring planes and rescue ships. We had only to move toward land and wait. I tied the rope to my kapok life jacket and, pulling my cans behind me, swam slowly on my back toward the unknown island. Several times waves rolled over my head and I fought back the water, gasping. Frequently, I stopped to rest, to judge my distance and direction. The land seemed no closer. The night was a long one.

I thought I had never seen a more beautiful dawn. The bright color swept up quickly after the first glimmer, clear pink and rose and a line of green. A feeling of relief surged through me. Here was light and increased warmth and possibility of rescue.

Turning my head, I saw not one but three green islands. The closest was Savo Island with its volcanic peak, and beyond, Florida and Guadalcanal. Far to my right, seven or eight hundred yards away, I could make out two men on an inflated pillow or mattress cover. Another man floated some four hundred yards to my left. I called out. The man to my left waved. But I saw no one else. Currents around the islands are strong and often irregular. The others might be far away by now or just beyond my line of vision. I could see the *Duncan* drifting low in the water, her fires still burning.

Breaking in on the quiet lapping of the water, a faint buzzing began, like distant swarm of bees. It increased steadily. Watching the sky to the south, I saw a neat pattern of 100 to 150 planes very high. They must have taken off from the field on Guadalcanal for dawn patrol, and since I had been uncertain of the outcome of the fighting on the island, I felt reassured. Surely, too, on their return a few would fly lower and see us. I lay on my back, relaxed, appreciating the clean formation of planes against the sky, judging their number.

At this moment, I felt a scratching, tickling sensation in my left foot.

Slightly startled, I pulled it out of the water and held it up. It was gushing blood.

What had caused it? I jerked my head around to the left, peering into the water.

Close to the surface, not ten feet away, I saw the glistening brown back of a great fish. He was swimming away. What was he? I think I knew immediately, but my mind would not accept it.

Would he keep going or would he turn and come back? Had he deliberately attacked me, or had he only brushed against my bare foot accidentally? What weapon could I use? I had no knife. I had thrown away my pistol because of its weight. I had nothing—nothing but my bare hands and feet.

The real fear did not hit me until I saw him turn and head back toward me. He didn't rush. His 5-foot body, breaking the surface of the water, came in a steady direct line, effortless and deadly. I kicked and splashed tremendously and this time he veered off past me, not frightened, not hurrying.

Now I grabbed my powder cans and thrust one under each knee to keep my feet up. I yanked at my life jacket, raising it to lift my body further out of the water.

All the time I followed him with my eyes. He went out about 20 feet and swam back and forth.

I shouted to the man to my left, "Have you got a knife?" There was no answer.

The shark was going to come in. Every muscle in my body tensed for the attack. He waited, as if he knew the terrible toll of waiting on the victim. With a great effort, I yelled to the men far off to my right: "A shark! Have you a knife? A knife?"

Then he turned to make the attack. He came in from the same angle toward my left. I raised my right arm, holding it up as I watched him come and trying to control myself. When he was almost upon me, I thrashed out, kicking and splashing. I brought my fist down on his nose with all my force again and again. He was thrust down into the water about two feet. He swam by and I saw him go out and stay there, waiting.

I looked myself over and discovered that he had torn off a piece of my left hand.

I tried to shout to the men again. "A shark! A shark's eating me! Have you a knife?" I kept repeating it, and the effort was wearing me out. Finally they waved back. No, they had no knife.

I realized that I would have to save my strength. If he was going to keep on attacking, I would have to make myself rest between attacks so that I could hit him hard enough at the right moment. But could I keep it up?

I lay waiting for him. About fifteen minutes must have passed. Then I saw him start to come in, again at the same angle to my left.

When his head was almost upon me, his jaw plainly visible beneath, I brought my fist down across my body and managed to hit him on the eyes, the nose. The flesh was torn from my left arm. He passed me and as he did so I could feel the movement of his great body against me.

My whole mind and body now centered on the battle against annihilation, as if I were an animal fighting off a stronger, larger beast. At intervals of ten or fifteen minutes he would ease off from his slow swimming and bear directly toward me, coming in at my left.

Only twice did he go beneath me. Helpless against this type of attack, I feared it most, but because I was so nearly flat on top of the water, he seemed unable to get at me from below.

Each time he attacked on the surface I could hit him, but each time he took another nip out of me. After an attack, I would raise my feet and arms to see what I had left. The big toe on my left foot was dangling. A piece of my right heel was gone. My left elbow, hand, and calf were torn. If he did not actually sink his teeth into me, his rough hide would scrape off great pieces of my skin. The salt water staunched the flow of blood somewhat and I was not conscious of great pain. The physical shock of the encounter served to keep that in check for a while.

During one scuffle, the lid of one of the powder cans came off. I snatched at it but the can filled immediately and sank. Quickly, I shifted my position to rest both knees on the remaining can. Once I glanced off toward the Duncan. She was no longer there. She had sunk and I had not even seen her go down.

Time was incalculable, endless. I knew I was slowly losing the battle. My concentration never wavered, but my strength was going. The constant hitting with my right fist made the muscular ache in my arm more painful than my wounds.

Then I heard the planes again. The dawn patrol was returning to Guadalcanal. About a dozen planes flew at low altitude, zooming over me. Surely they would see me. I made frantic motions. I wave and yelled. I saw three or four pilots wave their white scarves at me as they flew by.

Again, I faced the shark, hope now making my blows more savage.

As I lay there watching, I looked up and, suddenly, there was a ship approaching. Was it American or Japanese? I had no idea who had won the battle. Squinting my eyes against the brilliance of the sun which was now high in the sky, I finally made out that it was a U.S. destroyer. They were coming for me. First the men nearer to them. Then me. Then me.

I turned my eyes away with a great effort, to watch the shark. When I could look back again their boat was nearer. I yelled and shouted, but they were still too far away to hear. Then the lifeboat was within a couple of hundred yards, full of survivors. I tore off my undershirt and waved it wildly. The boat turned and I was sure no one had seen me. I kept yelling. Then I controlled myself, feeling that they were only going back to the destroyer with that boatload. They would be back for me. I had only to wait a little, to fight once more. They would come back, I was certain.

I saw the boat return to the ship and disappear on the far side. In numb silence, I saw the ship get way upon her. She hoisted in her boat. She came in my direction at high speed. I screamed again and again. She passed me. No one had seen me. They were leaving me, leaving me to the shark.

In the excitement, I had forgotten the shark. Now he was upon me before I was ready. I fought him off, swinging my arms, hitting blindly. I turned and whirled and struck. As he swam away, I lifted my left leg. He had torn out the flesh in my thigh so deeply that the bone was exposed.

Fumbling and weak, I started to try to make a tourniquet out of my shirt but gave up. A tourniquet would make the leg numb and I needed it to fight with. I struggled against passing out.

I tried to recapture the control I had previously achieved between attacks but now the idea of getting out of my life jacket began to grow on me. How much quicker it would be! I fingered the fastenings clumsily. How much easier! They had gone away and left me.

But the body will keep on fighting even when the will is going, and even a small man has tremendous strength in desperation.

Another plane came over. I hardly heard him as he zoomed low. I tried to wave and it seemed to require a terrible effort. Everything seemed hazy and confused.

Then the shark came in again, and I must have struck back at him automatically.

When I finally raised my head, there, unbelievably, was a destroyer coming toward me at about 20 knots. It was now nearly noon. The ship might have noticed the plane diving over my position. I snatched my shirt and tried to wave. Floundering in the water, I raised the powder can and held it up, thinking that perhaps the sun would shine on it.

It fell back in the water and I waved both arms. I shouted. Perhaps I was only seeing things. Or again, maybe they would not see me. There were men on the forward part. Why didn't they wave back? They were coming right toward me. Perhaps they would run me down and never know I was here.

And then, one man on top of Gun No. 2 waved. He was waving both arms at me.

I started to paddle furiously. All my strength seemed to come back and I thought I was swimming toward them at a great rate. With those strong strokes, I thought any moment now I would be bumping the side of the ship. I stopped and took a look. I had made no headway whatsoever.

The men on the deck were cheering. They had seen the shark. Usually, if a man is in the water, the procedure is to tie a line to a strong swimmer and send him out but they obviously could not do that. As I paddled futilely, I heard a zing close to my head and looked up again. Five or six men were lined up on the deck above me with rifles, shooting at the shark.

A terrible fear of being shot to death in the water, when rescue was so near, swept over me. With each zing of a bullet, I screamed and pleaded and cried out to them to stop. The shark was too close. They would hit me first.

Then the firing ceased. A small boat came toward me. I remember them reaching out and the feel of someone's arms as I was dragged over the gunwale. I collapsed in the bottom of the boat, vomiting. Someone kept saying that it didn't matter. I asked about the other men in the water. Had they found them too?

An officer bent over me as I called for morphine. I could hear him repeat, "Herb, you're all right now. You're all right, Herb."

I looked at his face. By some strange chance, he was a friend to whom I had said goodbye only a few months before in Jersey City.

A seaman tied a tourniquet around my leg. I was still conscious. I could see my friend's face above me again as they gave me morphine. "Other men in the water," I was saying, but I couldn't seem to make out their answer. I passed out.

I have spent fourteen months in a hospital ship, a base and a U.S. hospital. The scars are still deep, but I was fortunate, amazingly fortunate.

One thing I do know. The human body is a wonderful mechanism. It will fight against great odds and take terrible punishment. It can call up strength you never imagined it possessed. Men on every battlefield and ocean must be discovering this and feeling the same surprise and wonderment that I did.

MONA ISLAND

George A. Llano

*Juan Suarez-Morales, a librarian, is worked over by a shark, narrowly
escapes death, and then suggests, to the boatman who delivered him, something so terrifically ridiculous that no shark attack collection is complete
without including this account. We can only hope that on his return to the
library, Sr. Suarez-Morales thumbed into a book or two on common sense.*

On Saturday, July 5, 1952, Señor Juan Suarez-Morales, then
Librarian of the University of Puerto Rico at Mayaguez,
decided to go spearfishing off Mona Island, which lies
some 50 miles east of Puerto Rico. On this particular
morning, the land temperature was about eighty-eight degrees Fahrenheit and the crystal-clear water was relatively warm.

Wearing a yellow bathing suit, a white polo shirt, blue fins, mask,
and snorkel, and armed with a spearfishing gun, Señor Morales entered
the sea about 7:30 A.M. For the first hour and a half, he poked around an
area of reefs and shoals back with a multitude of small fish which had
already attracted schools of several species of larger fish. His first shot got
him a large shad which he carried to the beach. He then returned to the
shoals to resume his sport.

At this time, approximately 9:00 A.M., Morales became aware of the
presence of a shark which apparently had followed him toward the shore,
probably attracted by the struggles of the speared shad. The shark, estimated by the hunter to be about 5 feet long, had clean-swept lines and
was colored dark above and white below. However, it gave him no concern and he shooed it away with a wave of his spear.

Continuing his fishing, Morales missed his second shot and was
forced to dive to recover his spear. At this time, about ten minutes after
his first kill, "I had the sensation that something was behind me," wrote
Morales. "And indeed, it was 'el Señor Tiburon' ready to leap forward."

But, with a rapid movement of his spear gun, Morales frightened the shark away. He went on fishing, albeit with growing caution, spearing a five-pound mackerel, which he fastened to his belt. During this interval, the shark was seen repeatedly in the offing until about 10:00 A.M. when it disappeared. Shortly thereafter, Morales' spearhead became loosened and he decided to return to the dock a distance across the water of about 150 yards. Because of the weight of his catch, now tied to the useless spear gun, and the awkwardness of walking with fins, he decided to swim back, parallel to the shore.

"At the start, I again encountered the shark. I recall that I was worried by such an assiduous bodyguard and having no other weapon, I threw a couple of stones at him to chase him away. I decided to walk a little in order to fool the shark. After walking a good stretch, I threw myself into the sea and swam about 30 feet from shore in water between 10 and 12 feet deep. Once, the fish came loose and floated on the water several feet away. I went after them and secured them better. From time to time and in between small rests, I could already see the dock. A few minutes more and the task would be ended." It was now almost 11:00 A.M.

"In this area, there are rocks near the shore so I had to swim out somewhat. I was pushing the fish ahead of me as I swam. Then, without warning, I felt as if I had been struck by a rocket or as if an animal was repeatedly jumping on me. It was the shark which, coming up from behind, had seized me by the knee. I felt no pain, no fear, no panic." There was no time to call for help because the shark's lunge pulled Morales violently to the bottom.

"I was wearing a mask and snorkel, which helped me a great deal since I could actually see my enemy and fight him the best I could without swallowing too much water. I released my load and tried to fight the shark by punching him on the nose with my fist, but the animal would not let go. . . . Then came to me—like a flash—the idea of pushing into the eyes of my enemy. . . . As soon as I pressed down on those far-apart, hard eyes, the shark let go, disappearing in a cloud of blood. I made land in no time." And by shouting in English, then Spanish, Morales succeeded in attracting help.

"The wound was deep and lacerated with a bone fracture on the right side below the knee." Morales estimated that the attack lasted about sixty seconds. At this time "when the shark seized, I sort of laughed to myself on the futility of life. . . . I thought that if the shark snapped off my leg, I should get rid of my mask and snorkel and swallow water to avoid a slow and painful death. . . ." After reaching shore, Morales said, he tried to walk but could not, adding: "I don't think I was scared to the point of shock. . . ." While being ferried to the dock, Morales asked the boatman to go by the place of the attack to see if he could recover his spear gun and fish. The man refused—"obstinately."

A KILLER GETS SOME RESPECT

Michael Tennesen

Following a series of fatal shark attacks in Hawaiian waters during the 1990s, scientists took a studied look at the situation, and their findings helped dispel some long-standing myths about tiger sharks (they estimated that the odds of being attacked by a shark in Hawaiian waters is roughly one in 5 million). This was little consolation for the precious few who'd been attacked, but it underscored for the rest of us that such attacks, be they in Hawaii or anywhere else, are rare events indeed.

Louise Sourisseau was snorkeling with her friend Martha Morrell on the Hawaiian island of Maui when Sourisseau felt the rough skin of a tiger shark dragging across her calf. Sourisseau watched in horror as the 10-foot-long shark swam past her and repeatedly attacked her friend, biting off both her legs and an arm. Morrell, the forty-two-year-old wife of a plantation owner, died instantly on that November day in 1991.

Less than a year later, eighteen-year-old Aaron Romento was body surfing on Oahu when a tiger shark appeared and bit him in three places on the right leg. Surfers nearby pulled him ashore but the bites had severed Romento's femoral artery, and he bled to death before they could get him to the hospital.

These two fatalities, coupled with six other confirmed shark attacks in Hawaii from 1991 to 1992, triggered media frenzy. Shark sightings were front-page news in Hawaiian newspapers, along with photos of shark hunters hoisting catches as vengeance for the human deaths. A bill was introduced in the Hawaiian legislature to initiate a $200,000 program to send more hunters after the animals.

The initial response to the Hawaiian shark attacks was much the same as in the late 1950s, when tiger sharks killed a surfer. Back then the state launched a $300,000 program to get even, and nearly 4,700 sharks of several species died as a result. But many things had changed in the intervening three decades, causing legislators to pause this time. One change was a new awareness of and respect for Native Hawaiian beliefs, which viewed certain tiger sharks as sacred *aumakua,* or guardian spirits. There was also a new ecological consciousness that included respect for the ocean and its wild denizens. And there was a dawning awareness of the plight of sharks, millions of which die in commercial fisheries each year for each human that is reported killed by a shark.

Another key to the bill's eventual defeat was the role of wildlife biologists, in particular fifty-one-year-old Kim Holland, an associate researcher at the Hawaii Institute of Marine Biology. Holland pointed out that the basic biology of tiger sharks was not well understood a decade ago. "We didn't know if shark control would do any good," says Holland, a native of England who moved to Hawaii. "The scientific community could not give sound answers as to whether or not a limited, focused fishing effort could in fact have any chance of catching the shark or sharks that did the dirty deed."

Holland and a group of graduate students, including Brad Wetherbee and Chris Lowe from the University of Hawaii, decided to look into this question shortly after the attacks in the early 1990s. The answers they found have helped to dispel some long-standing myths about tiger sharks and are leading to a less hostile attitude toward the fish in Hawaii and elsewhere.

Tiger sharks (so-called because they are striped, a feature most prevalent in juveniles) are found all over the world in tropical and temperate waters. On the Atlantic coast, the species ranges from Massachusetts in the north to Uruguay in the south. On the Pacific coast, it is found from Southern California to Peru. The creature is one of about 400 species of sharks worldwide, ranging from the deepwater 10-inch-long dwarf shark to the 40-foot-long whale shark. Several of these species are capable of biting a human, but Great White sharks, bull sharks, and tiger sharks are responsible for 99 percent of attacks, according to the International Shark Attack File.

Holland feels the public fear of sharks is unwarranted, however.

There were twenty-six shark attacks from 1990 to 1997 in Hawaii with three fatalities, compared to forty fatal drownings each year in Hawaiian waters. With 20 million people entering Hawaiian waters each year, the odds of being attacked by a shark are about one in five million. What's more, only about one-fifth of those attacked by sharks worldwide are killed. Apparently sharks do not like the taste of human flesh. "Tiger sharks are efficient hunters," says Holland. "If sharks liked human flesh, we'd see a lot more fatalities."

To get more information about tiger sharks, especially their movements and home ranges, Holland and his fellow researchers needed to get transmitters on some of the fish. So they started setting fishing lines for sharks offshore near Honolulu International Airport. Thirty-yard leaders baited with fish heads were attached to a main line about 400 yards long. Tiger sharks hooked on these leaders could keep swimming—vital to the creatures since they must move to breathe. The baited lines brought in an average of one tiger shark a night.

To tag the animals, the biologists used an 18-foot Boston whaler that was not much bigger than some of the sharks they captured (which ranged from 7 to 14 feet in length). Hooked sharks were brought alongside the whaler, restrained with ropes and then flipped over. Once turned over, the tiger shark would go into a trancelike condition called tonic immobility. This allowed the biologists to surgically implant a transmitter without using an anesthetic. When completed, the hook was removed and the shark released.

The biologists noted that female tiger sharks had may scars on their backs. These wounds are usually a side effect of mating, when males restrain females by biting them on the back and fins. Both male and female sharks have thick hides, however; one researcher describes the skin of a tiger shark as being six to ten times the tensile strength of ox hide.

Sharks are equipped with several rows of teeth that when lost are replaced rapidly. (Some species of sharks may lose as many as 30,000 teeth during their lives.) Behind those teeth are powerful jaws armed with elastic muscles, which enables the fish to distend its mouth and swallow huge pieces of food. In Australia, one 11-foot tiger shark was found with an entire horse's head, intact, inside its stomach.

Although horse's heads are not a staple of the tiger shark's diet, the creatures do have wide-ranging tastes. Smaller sharks eat mostly fish, along with birds, but as tiger sharks grow larger their diet switches to dolphins, other sharks, and rays. Tiger sharks also go after seemingly inedible prey such as puffer fish, stingrays, triggerfish, and sea snakes. Researchers aren't sure how the sharks survive the barbs, bites, and stings of these prickly prey.

Tiger sharks have a variety of sensors for locating prey. Like other sharks, they have a line of vibration detectors located along their sides that enable them to pick up the pressure waves of a moving animal. The sharks also use special organs below the skin of their snouts that allow them to detect faint electrical fields generated by living creatures. Sometimes the sharks pick up the electrical fields generated by motors and mistake them for prey, however. Bill Gilmartin, a federal government biologist who studied Hawaiian monk seals, reported a 12-foot tiger shark that burst out of the water behind his boat and engulfed the propeller with its jaws, lifting the entire craft.

Holland's crew got used to tiger sharks banging up against its boat. The researchers tagged some 200 sharks and fitted forty with transmitters that could be tracked by boats or listening devices set on the ocean floor. What the transmitters revealed was that tiger sharks travel long distances for their food.

All of the tiger sharks tracked swam more than 10 miles offshore in the first twenty-four hours after release and did not return to the area during the following forty-eight hours. It was not unusual for one of these fish to cover 30 to 40 miles a day. And though they eventually revisited monitoring sites, they did so on an irregular basis, with intervals ranging anywhere from two weeks to ten months.

The implication of this discovery was that if tiger sharks don't stay close to one area, "It makes no sense to kill sharks in the vicinity of an attack and expect to solve the problem," Holland says.

The local news media gave extensive coverage to Holland's findings, and that helped quell the call for revenge in the Hawaiian legislature. Not everyone was happy with the idea of letting the sharks off, however. "If we had thirty people attacked in the last ten years by wild dogs in Ala Moana Park [a seaside park near Honolulu], how many wild dogs would be in Ala Moana Park?" asked Jim Cook, chairman of the Western Pacific Fishery Management Council.

Surprisingly, another reason for the defeat of the legislation was a call for moderation from shark bite survivors. Honolulu author Greg Ambrose interviewed ten victims of tiger shark attacks for his book *Shark Bites* and was amazed at the epiphany each had. "In every case the tiger shark actually had their teeth upon them and was biting into their flesh, but let them go," wrote Ambrose. "The lesson they learned was that the shark didn't want the people, that their mighty fear of sharks had been totally unfounded. In most cases they've become eloquent spokespersons for sharks."

One of those victims was Jonathan Mozo, a photographer who lives out on Oahu. On the morning of June 10, 1993, he was surfing at Goats, a spot on the north shore. Suddenly, he felt a piercing pain and crushing pressure on his lower legs. He looked back and saw his feet and his board in the mouth of a tiger shark. As he watched, the animal opened its mouth and swam forward for a bigger bite. Mozo screamed, yanked his feet out of the creature's mouth, and paddled to shore as fast as he could. His friends put tourniquets around his ankles to keep him from bleeding to death, as surfer Aaron Romento had done a few months earlier. It took more than 100 stitches to sew Mozo back up, but he was surfing again only two months later.

Mozo expresses the feelings of many Hawaiians who have now come to accept the tiger shark as part of the marine environment. "I have no feelings of hatred against the shark," he says. "I don't want revenge. I don't think they should be eliminated. We are not the masters of [the] sea. If it were our territory we'd have been born with gills and fins. I was out there a guest in his world. I just feel lucky he let me live."

SHARK ATTACK/MONTEREY

Kief Hillsbery

During Christmas week, 1981, surfer Lew Boren paddled out into the streaming combers at Asilomar beach in Monterey, California, much as he had done a thousand times before. "The next day his bloodstained board washed up at Asilomar with a 17-inch semicircular hole, deep and perfectly outlined," writes Hillsbery in the following story, which tries to plug a few facts into that gaping hole, as well as rounding out the profile of the "hound of the sea," the formidable Great White shark.

We all grew up surfing in southern California, and sharks were there but not there. The water was the place to be, and what mattered in the water was to stay, just a little bit longer. Another wave, another set, another green-glass morning apart from the world. We all knew about sharks. But all we knew for sure was the surge of adrenaline when kelp brushed against our legs while we waited in the lineup.

So we called the Great White the Landlord, and we smiled when we said it. No American surfer had ever been killed by a shark. No one pointed out that the rent was overdue.

A decade or so ago—before *Jaws*—a survey was conducted in Australia to determine what single word had the greatest emotional impact on the respondents. Rape. Murder. Poison. Death. Love. Sex. Snake. The word that hit home hardest was *shark.*

Almost every large-animal predator on land has been eliminated or confined, but two-thirds of the planet belongs to the shark. Sharks are survivors. They have patrolled the oceans for 350 million years and they have changed very little. Sharks were in the water long before the appearance of man. Today there are around 350 species: deep-water sharks and surface sharks, coastal sharks and oceanic sharks, arctic sharks and tropical sharks. They are one of the most numerous carnivores on earth, and in the hierarchy of aquatic killers, the Great White shark reigns supreme.

The Great White is the Hound of the Sea. White Death, the last undefeated man-eater left. It measures up to 25 feet long, weighs as much as 5 tons, and possesses enormous jaws and row upon row of serrated, razor-sharp teeth. The Great White's brain is the size of a six-pack, and its sensory organs are among the most acute in the animal kingdom. It can see a hundred feet in clear water, pick up the sound of unusual movements a hundred yards away, and follow a diffuse odor trail a mile distant. It seems to home in on its prey for the last 2 or 3 feet through detection of faint bioelectric signals, and once the signals are received, the Great White is insatiable. It will eat anything in the water: pet bulldogs, license plates, kegs of nails, and gunnysacks of "shark repellent." Not to mention turtles, porpoises, and man.

Lew Boren hated crowds. He liked to surf alone, and his idea of perfection was empty azure water at dawn, with sage-scented offshore winds blowing down the coastal canyons. On mornings like that, nothing could spoil the fine, smooth symbiosis of mind, muscle, and wave. No noise, no jostling for position. But in southern California today there are very few mornings like that.

The surfers call it localism: "If you don't live here, don't surf here." There is a finite number of waves, an infinite number of board riders, and the only way to stay on top is to push people around. If they come from more than a mile away, they are geeks. Invaders. Kooks. Surfers spear one another with surfboards and settle up in the courtroom instead of on the beach. Assault with a deadly weapon. A thousand dollars and a year in jail. Fun, fun, fun.

Lew Boren was born in 1957, the year the first plastic foam-core surfboards came on the market. He grew up on 232nd Street in Torrance, one of the smog-shrouded flatland suburbs south of Los Angeles International Airport, where the sea breezes are blocked by the Palos Verdes Hills, where the neighboring towns of Lomita, Gardena, and

Lawndale merge into one another like cloning amoebas, where the listless palms and rows of stucco bungalows suggest nothing so much as ennui. But when Lew was five years old something happened. The Beach Boys borrowed a Chuck Berry tune to tell the world that "If everybody had an ocean Across the USA Then everybody'd be surfin' like Californ-i-ay" and it wasn't long before the woodies and Chevys and bushy blond hairdos gave Pacific Coast Highway the aspect of a pilgrim's way. By the time he turned twelve, Lew was ditching school and taking the bus to Redondo Beach, 5 miles from Torrance, light years from 232nd Street. The beach was speed and style and endless summer. The beach was where Lew Boren belonged.

And the beach was where he stayed, even when the crowds got bad and the sport turned mean. Even when he could check out the quality of surf by the quantity of cars in the parking lot. Even when surfing meant a three-hour drive north to the Hollister Ranch, where the Santa Ynez Mountains drop down to one of the last undeveloped chunks of private coastal real estate in southern California.

But when Lew graduated from Torrance High in 1975, he began to consider his options. He tried El Camino Community College. He tried the beaches of Baja. And then he loaded up his third-hand truck and headed north of Highway 1, bound for Monterey where the twisted pines and cypresses fringe the clear, cold bay like an overgrown bonsai forest, where a hundred-odd surfers share a 50-mile stretch of coastline, where six men and one woman had been attacked by sharks in the space of twenty years.

Perhaps 10 percent of all species of sharks are potential man-eater, and most of them are included in the group called lamnoids. Lamnoids vary in size but in their apparent single-mindedness they are remarkably alike.

Take sand tiger sharks, which begin eating before they are born. Researchers dissecting female sand tigers were shocked to discover the remains of sibling sharks in the bellies of embryos, conclusive evidence of "intrauterine cannibalism."

Take the Great White shark which returns to hit off victims again and again, ignoring the commotion of rescue attempts and even the dangling limbs of rescuers. Until 1982 the only fatality out of seven shark attacks in Monterey County was Barry Wilson, a seventeen-year-old swimmer who was already missing the flesh from his left leg from calf to thigh when four skin divers fitted him with an inflatable collar and began towing him to shore. Undeterred, the Great White attacked again, taking another bite from between Wilson's legs. Following closely, it moved in for more flesh whenever the rescuers stopped swimming. The divers were unharmed but Wilson died within a minute after he was laid on the sand, his thigh bones laid bare and his femoral arteries severed.

Which is why the classification lamnoid owes its name to the mythical Greek monster Lamia, who could only be appeased by the sacrifice of a handsome young athlete. Which is why the eighteenth-century naturalist Linnaeus believed that the monster that swallowed Jonah was not a whale but a Great White shark. Which is why the French word for shark—*requin*—derives from Requiem, the Mass for the Dead.

When Lew Boren found a place in Monterey, he put the Doors on the stereo and sprouts in the Frigidaire and a life-size poster of Jimi Hendrix on the bedroom wall. "He became a good friend to a lot of the young surfers because he was mellow," remembers Patty Stember Kintz, who lived with Lew on Eardley Street in Pacific Grove. "They just couldn't imagine being mellow, but they wanted to be mellow, so Lew was just incredible."

Lew *was* incredible, a Sixties person in an Eighties world, who told his friends that all he wanted out of life was good waves and good smoke, whose plan for the future came down to surfing his brains out and eventually ending up in Oregon, where he'd kick back, grow pot and smoke it. He liked Monterey because the herb from Carmel Valley was plentiful and potent, and because there were always waves somewhere, at Asilomar or Carmel Bay, Moss Landing or Molera, at any one of a dozen rock reefs or beach breaks. In Monterey, Lew could have waves to himself, and he could have the old-time camaraderie, the endless communal cruise on Highway 1, every oncoming car with surf racks spreading the word:

thumbs up, surf's up; thumbs down, no waves. The house on Eardley Street became a haven for anyone who surfed and needed a place to stay, and although the parties were never rowdy, they always lasted late.

"I was working the graveyard shift at a bread maker's," says Patty, "and I'd come home in the morning and there'd be surf guys on my bed, on my rug and in the living room. And I'd get all upset and scream and decide to move out, and Lew would say, 'Just mellow out, Patty. Mellow out.'"

Patty finally did move out, not long after Lew rented a big old beat-up camper shell for his truck and took to sleeping at the surfing breaks, the better to catch two or three hours' worth of morning waves before he punched the clock at Terra Engineering, near Fisherman's Wharf, where he worked as a machinist. Lew's wheels were dubbed the Tiltin' Hilton and they gave him the freedom he craved.

"No one to take care of and no one to answer to, that was his ideal," says Patty. "I'd talk about getting married, and he'd just shake his head. He just couldn't imagine ever doing anything like that. He had to have people, but he didn't want them close.

"Above all else, he had to surf."

A shark out of water is a shark condemned to death. Its skin distends and its internal organs are torn apart by the effect of their own weight, which ordinarily is supported by water pressure outside the thin abdominal wall. Deprived of its support for more than the briefest period, the shark dies.

Its reproductive system is primitive but specialized. Unlike most other fish, the male shark possesses two claspers, elongated extensions of the pelvic fins that function as dual penises during mating. Breading is a matter of a group of sharks gathering and milling around, a lone female racing away and a male giving chase. He signals his intentions by biting the female's flanks and fins.

Two-thirds of all sharks have live young, commonly from six to twelve at one time, after a gestation period ranging from ten months to two years. The pups immediately begin feeding. The closest a female shark comes to nourishing her offspring is to abstain from feeding for several days in the area where she gave birth, a protective mechanism that prevents the shark from consuming her own pups.

Except for their sudden and violent courtship, sharks are solitary creatures. They live alone, although they do travel in loose aggregations. They spend much of their lives sampling the water for traces of blood and awaiting the faint vibrations that indicate a nearby animal in trouble. When they sense prey, sharks become progressively more excited, weaving from side to side as they approach, circling the object of interest until satisfied that an attack is safe. The shark then throws itself upon its prey with such ferocity that other sharks in the vicinity are drawn by the pressure waves, and in the ensuing feeding frenzy, the water boils with blood and snapping jaws. When the food is gone the sharks disperse in an instant and resume their ceaseless solitary patrol.

The search for food is not the only reason for their constant motion. Most sharks, including the Great White, lack a "swimming bladder," the organ that enables other fish to stabilize themselves at different depths. If a shark stops swimming, it sinks to the bottom. Most larger sharks also lack a mechanism for pumping water over their gills; their respiration is dependent upon movement through the water. Sharks are survivors, but they have to keep moving in order to survive.

Lew Boren had to surf, but the way that he surfed was on his knees. It wasn't long after he came north that he decided to stay in Monterey and stopped talking about Oregon. In Monterey he could surf wherever he wanted, and no one gave him any shit about not standing up.

Most surfers regard kneeboarders as kooks. But when the subject comes up at Eleventh Street in Carmel, the most reliable springtime surfing break on the Monterey Peninsula, they're willing to make an exception in the case of Lew Boren.

"With his little kneeboard and two fins, he could line up and catch any wave," say Lew's buddy Steve Miller. "Any big wave. Any size wave that a surfer with a 7-foot-plus surfboard could catch. And that's really something to say."

Lew was always out on the biggest days and he did a lot of things that other people wouldn't do, like running the gate on Seventeen-Mile Drive. Lew never felt right if he went into work without checking out the surf on the Drive. The Drive was bleak and rock-bound, flooded with inexhaustible fog, and when the waves weren't there, the wildness was enough. The only problem with the Drive was the four-dollar toll, and Patty would call the gate guard every morning and give a phony name and say she lived in Pebble Beach and was expecting Lew Boren. It worked really well until Patty ran out of believable names. The guards got wise and Lew was barred from the Drive; his only option was running the gate.

Which turned out to be easy. He'd slide right through with a wave and a smile, cruise around a corner and park so he could see the waves through the trees in his rear-view mirror. He'd watch the guards roar down the Drive, and he'd laugh and light a big one, then check the surf and head for Monterey. They never figured it out, not for three weeks running, not until a sheriff's deputy appeared at the house on Eardley Street with a couple of warrants and asked, "Are you Lew Boren? Does a girl named Bella Abzug live here?"

He had to surf but he never stood up. One day Patty asked him why, and Lew said he didn't want to. He said he liked being close to the wave. He said he just wanted to hug the wave.

Fewer than 500 deaths in all of recorded history have been attributed to shark attacks. But most authorities believe that a large number of fatalities in Africa, Asia, and South America go unreported, and even in densely populated areas of Australia and the United States, scores of people disappear while diving or swimming. Some "deaths by drowning" may involve attacks by sharks; how many is anyone's guess.

More than any other large wild animal, the shark is a mystery. "We just don't know very much," says Stewart Springer, for forty years one of the work's leading shark researchers. "Particularly with the Great Whites, very little research has been done because they're hard as the devil to handle. They've never been tagged or tracked, and we don't even know how many there are."

Even the way a shark's jaw works has long been misunderstood.

Because its teeth are located far beneath its protruding snout, it had been believed that the shark could only seize flesh with its belly thrust forward. But recent underwater photography supervised by the Cousteaus revealed that when a shark opens its mouth to eat, its lower jawbone shoots forward and its snout draws up almost perpendicular to its body. With its jaw jutting out and up, the shark's head resembles a gargantuan wolf trap, studded with scores of gleaming teeth. By applying the entire weight of its body in a series of convulsive thrashing movements, the shark transforms its jawbones into saws.

"The force of this sawing effect," says Jacques-Yves Cousteau, "is such that it requires no more than an instant for a shark to tear off a splendid morsel of flesh. When the shark swims off, he has left a deep and perfectly outlined hole in the body of its victim."

But not to worry. The shark researchers tend to agree that man is an unusual food for sharks. Reports Eugenie Clark, professor of zoology at the University of Maryland: "During twenty-six years of research on sharks, I have found them to be normally unaggressive and even timid toward man. With the sole exception of the Great White shark." The Landlord.

Dawn at the Drive, December 20th, 1981. Low visibility, rain on the horizon, 7-, 8- and 9-foot waves at Spanish Bay, the most exposed surfing break between Santa Cruz and Point Lobos. Lew Boren and Bruce McNaughton sat in the Tiltin' Hilton, eating cereal and checking the surf.

Bruce remembers deciding not to go out that day because the swell was too large. He remembers asking Lew if it was true that he'd surfed Point Sur alone. Lew said that it was, and he'd never seen any killer waves come through. Never mind that two of the three recovered shark attacks on California surfers had occurred at Point Sur.

Bruce watched Lew paddle out and disappear into the fog bank, with the waves pounding and the stratus building and the rain was just beginning. Lew didn't come back. The next day, his blood-stained board washed up at Asilomar with a 17-inch semicircular hole, deep and perfectly outlined.

The headlines in Monterey during Christmas week of 1981 were not exactly soothing if all you cared about was looking for a ride. GIANT SHARK ATTACKED SURFBOARD, SAYS SCIENTIST. SHARK ATTACKS LIKELY TO INCREASE. The regular, triangular marks in Lew Boren's surfboard spelled shark bite, the spacing spelled monster.

"It was definitely a white shark, possibly the largest so far on this coast," announced marine biologist Daniel Miller of the California Department of Fish and Game. "These bites are the largest I've every seen." Miller and the other shark experts agreed that the shark that hit Lew's board measured from 18½ to 23 feet in length and weighed over 2 tons. Not as big as the 30-footer immortalized in *Jaws,* not as big as the 39-footer reportedly caught off Hawaii in the 1930s and not as big as *Carcharodon megalodon,* the prehistoric Great White whose fossilized teeth were originally classified as "viper's teeth" and "fossil birds' tongues" because naturalists could not conceive of an 80-foot shark. Take the long view, and the shark in Spanish Bay assumes the proportions of a pike.

But take the short view—Lew Boren, 6 foot 2, 180 pounds, brown hair and eyes, sea-gull tattoo on upper arm, last seen wearing black wet suit—and you get the hell out of the water.

Which is exactly what the California Department of Fish and Game had been recommending since October, when marine biologists noticed an increase in the number of white sharks in local waters and issued a general shark warning for the entire Monterey Bay area. With its fisheries, kelp beds, and rocky shoreline, the bay provides an ideal habitat for the seals and other pinnipeds that constitute the natural quarry of the Great White. Thanks to the Marine Mammals Protection Act of 1972, the elephant seal and the sea otter, which were close to extinction, are now flourishing. And as the pinnipeds go, say most authorities, so go the sharks.

In 1968, when University of California biology professor Burney Le Boeuf began keeping track of the seals on Año Nuevo Island, north of Santa Cruz, the colony numbered 460. Thirteen years later, the population had reached 4,000, and instead of finding three seal carcasses each season with evidence of shark bite, Le Boeuf was finding seventeen. And while there were eleven shark attacks on humans along the California-Oregon coast in the 1960s, there were twenty-two in the 1970s.

"We can expect more attacks because of an increase in the shark population," says Dr. John McCosker, director of the Steinhart Aquarium in San Francisco. "The number of elephant seals is increasing, so the number of white sharks will increase, and we will see more attacks because there is no decrease in the number of people in the water."

If Le Boeuf and McCosker are right, an unanswered question remains; why, with the surfeit of seal blubber in the immediate vicinity, does a twenty-foot shark home in on a solitary, sinewy surfer? The most common theory is mistaken identity. The black wet suit, the oblong board, the flippers flapping on the surface—to a cruising Great White, a surfer, and particularly a kneeboard surfer, presented a simulacrum of a seal.

But some scientists find the surfer-as-seal hypothesis unconvincing. Dr. H. David Baldridge, a retired navy captain who has analyzed the navy's international shark-attack file, told *Surfing* magazine he has seen "no data indicating that surfers as a group should be extracted from the normal beach population as being more susceptible to shark attack." Based on computer analysis of nearly 1,200 shark-attack incidents, Baldridge believes that up to 75 percent of all attacks on humans are not motivated by hunger. A more likely cause, says Baldridge, is a perceived threat; the shark is simply defending its territory. Call it localism.

There was a mean onshore wind blowing at Asilomar on the evening of December 22nd, and a bonfire blazing beacon-bright on the beach where Lew Boren's kneeboard had washed ashore the day before. Lew's body had not been found, but his mangled board was evidence enough for the hundred or so surfers who huddled close around the flames. They all looked very young, very Californian, with their white teeth and tangled blond hair, very much the embodiment of a particular dream from a particular time, the boys and girls of endless summer. But there they were, gathered in the cold on the edge of the continent, burning their surfboards in the traditional gesture of farewell, trying to say goodbye to someone they never really knew, "a guy who was basically a loner." There was beer and liquor and a eulogy and a prayer. There was talk of surfing Spanish Bay again, "when the waves are breaking right." And there was something very poignant about those golden inarticulate children who could speak of "the awesome and fearless power of the ocean" but could only say, when asked how they felt when they heard about Lew, that it was just like a movie.

At any given beach on any given day, the probability of a single shark attack is smaller than the probability of being struck by lightning, and the likelihood of multiple attacks by an insatiable rogue shark à la *Jaws* is right up there with the chances of a person's spending Christmas on Uranus. But the statistics were lost on the fortune hunters and the flacks, lured to Monterey no by the specter of a single mutilated surfer but by the prospects of mass hysteria and the main chance.

There was David Fisse, who described himself as a professional gold prospector and amateur diver. He promised to slay the killer shark even it if took him a month. Before Fisse made his first foray into the fifty-one-degree water of Monterey Bay, he posed for photographers with a .38-caliber bang stick. But he entered the water without a wet suit, and when Dane Burkland—playing Richard Dreyfuss to Fisse's Robert Shaw—attempted to rescue his hypothermic sidekick in their 18-foot aluminum launch, he couldn't get the motor started. An ABC camera crew sped up to the scene in a chartered party boat and ferried Fisse back to Fisherman's Wharf. He vowed to sell his house to finance the hunt.

There was Gerrit Klay, a veteran Florida shark hunter who claimed more than 4,000 catches with his partner, Charles Buie. Financed by Edward Montoro, president of the company distributing the film *Great White* ("Warning: intense scenes of overwhelming suspense require parental discretion"), Klay and Buie set sail from San Francisco in a twenty-ton spearfishing boat, intending to catch, tag, and track a Great White shark.

But a mammoth man-eater failed to appear. "I don't think there are any 20-footers," said Klay who hurried back to Florida, where at least the goddamned water was warm. David Fisse went home. And even the publicity couldn't save *Great White*, the advertising for which featured a drawing of a voluptuous woman lolling on an air mattress in the cavernous mouth of a man-eater. Ruling that the plot was so derivative it constituted an infringement of the *Jaws* copyright, Judge David Kenyon ordered the film withdrawn from distribution.

Life was imitating bad art, and imitating it badly. The surfers eventually returned to the water and the shark did not strike again. But when Lew Boren's surfboard washed up at Asilomar, it presaged an increase in the number of "cases": a fisherman killed off Tasmania, an elderly matron eaten alive off Palm Beach, a swimmer attacked north of San Francisco, all in the month of February, all by sharks.

Lew Boren hated crowds, and so did everyone else who surfed the breaks around Monterey. But things have changed since Lew disappeared. Steve Miller explains: "It used to be the people were really bummed with crowds, and now there's a completely different tone, of, like, the more the merrier. As far as most people are concerned, they'll accept crowds, especially in the Spanish Bay area. They realize that being out there alone is a lot spookier than being out with a bunch of people."

The more the merrier. More seals and other pinnipeds, more surfers who look like seals, more man-eating sharks. The trouble is, many Great White sharks live in the open sea and never venture close to shore. The vast majority of Great White sharks are scavengers and fish-eaters, and they attack humans only if humans are dumped into their environment through a shipwreck or plane crash. The vast majority of Great White sharks are what zoologist William Beebe had in mind when she termed the species "chinless cowards." But the vast majority does not include the sharks that Stewart Springer sometimes calls outcast.

Scientists don't know why most species of sharks—including the Great White—are divided into two distinct populations: a main breeding population and an excess or accessory, population. What seems clear is that the excess population is made up of loners, often deformed in some way. They abandon their home waters. They live in areas normally not visited by their own species. They never return to the usual shark breeding grounds. And sometimes what they do, at least in coastal waters, is kill people.

"An outcast is not necessarily a rogue," says Springer. "But it's reasonable to assume that the accessory population may be solely responsible for the increase in attacks on humans."

Fortunately, the outcast Great Whites are so widely dispersed that they have no opportunities to breed. They remain alone throughout their lives. Unless something happens. Unless an increase in the food supply can support a larger number of outcasts. More outcasts, more opportunities to breed—which makes things pretty dicey for people like Lew Boren.

Springer is a scientist, and he hesitates to draw conclusions without all the facts. But he thinks it's a possibility that the outcast sharks are breeding, and that they are defending their territories. The Landlords.

Lew Boren came to Monterey and lived the life he'd dreamed about in Los Angeles, the kind of wave-centered existence that for most surfers seems plausible enough at seventeen, but more than a little regressive at twenty-five. Like everyone else at the beach, Lew knew that surfing is essentially a young man's game, that localism is fast becoming the name of that game, that Monterey County is expected to gain another 100,000 people in the next fifteen years. He probably did not know about outcast sharks. But in any case, he had to surf. He was, his friends are quick to point out, an Aquarius. Lew believed, it is always made clear, in the endless summer. They found him in the fog at Asilomar on Christmas Eve with the left side of his torso ripped out from the hip to the armpit, dead in the water, on such a winter's day.

In the Jaws of a Shark

Peter Michelmore

"People do amazing things when they have to," said Dr. Andrew Nevitt, one of the ER docs who administered 200 sutures and 135 stainless steel staples to the shredded corpus of Eric Larsen, the shark attack survivor in the following story. In fact the doctor's words roundly describe the typical actions of all involved in a shark attack.

xcept for the seals bobbing their black heads in and out of the green Pacific waters, brothers Eric and Nick Larsen seemed to have the ocean to themselves.

Dressed in wet suits, gloves on their hands, they straddled their rocking surfboards under a brilliant blue sky. There was a southerly flow to the ocean this cool Monday morning, July 1, 1991. Four-foot waves were sweeping into a narrow, deserted beach, one of the many coves on the coastline north of California's Monterey Bay.

Sometime after 8:00 A.M., fifty-year-old Nick pointed his board toward the shore about 150 yards away. "I'm going to the truck to warm up," he said.

"I'll stay a little longer," Eric called after him.

Until ten weeks earlier, Eric had been a software engineer for a Silicon Valley company writing programs for a fiber-optic data network for the proposed NASA space station. But he found the pace too slow and wanted to be outdoors.

So when the company began laying off employees, the thirty-two-year-old told management he'd take a leave of absence. "That will mean one less person you have to let go." Life had been an athletic carnival since.

At 6 foot 1 and 175 pounds, Eric was always in shape. Now he brought himself to peak fitness, running, swimming, bicycling, board- and windsurfing and canoeing. Come fall, he would have to earn a living again, but for now he tried not to think about it.

• • •

Awaiting the break of a good wave, Eric gazed seaward. Then he noticed a swirling turbulence close by. *There's something really big down there,* he thought.

In that instant, he felt a powerful clamp on his left leg. Gaping in horror, he saw two wide rows of white, triangular teeth, bared to the gums, biting through flesh and muscle. Thigh to shin, his leg was caught in the jaws of a Great White shark at least 15 feet long.

Pry them loose! In lightning-fast reflex, Eric shot his gloved left hand to the top of the monster's snout, his right to the bottom. He pushed mightily against the jaws, while the shark tugged.

At that moment, the jaws opened, and Eric jerked his leg free. He kicked away from the hulking attacker, arms still outstretched. Too late, he tried to pull them in.

Lunging, tail thrashing, the shark sank its teeth deep into Eric's left arm from elbow to wrist and crunched down on the bone of the right forearm. His hands, untouched, groped inside the huge cavity of the mouth.

Eric was afraid, but not terrified. His engineer's mind focused on the trap-jaws. Pulling and tugging desperately, he felt his right arm move against the teeth. A fierce pull and he tore it out. *Attack! Hit him!* Bunching his right fist, he smashed the shark's gray-white belly in a hammer blow. The hide felt flat, muscular, but the pressure came off his left arm and he yanked it clear.

He was under the shark, away from its jaws. Then his body was jerked violently. The shark had snagged the six-foot nylon leash attaching Eric's right ankle to the surfboard. *I'm all chewed up,* he thought wildly, *and now this.*

For several seconds, he was towed through the water feet first at dizzying speed. Then, abruptly he was floundering. The leash was broken, the shark nowhere in sight.

He kicked to the surface and gulped air. His surfboard was floating only a few feet away, and he swung himself aboard, belly down.

Over the wave crests Eric caught a glimpse of the shoreline and paddled for it. *Relax,* he coached himself. *It's not over yet. Conserve your energy.*

He settled into a rhythmic pace, but each stroke of his arms left a scarlet trail. Anxiously, he scanned the ocean for a dorsal fin. The shark was out there somewhere. To find him, it had only to follow the blood.

Eric wanted to go faster, but dared not. The harder he paddled, the faster his heart pounded and the more blood he lost. Halfway to shore, he looked behind, and his eyes fixed on a wave rushing at him. Head up, hands guiding, he caught its crests and rode it to shore. *At least he can't get me here.*

A woozy feeling came over him as he sat there and inspected the raw pulp of tissue under the shreds of his wet suit. Down his left leg and along his arms were wounds that gaped to the bone. From the deep laceration above the knee, he judged that the shark had mangled the muscle. Blood spurted from a cut in the crook of his left arm. The shark had severed an artery. He had escaped its jaws, but now he could bleed to death in minutes.

He clamped the gash firmly with his right hand, and thrust the arm above his head. Blood must have been spouting out of the arm since the attack. Already the loss was making him faint.

Help lay about 200 yards to the north. He turned that way, dragging his left leg, until he was overcome by weakness and sank to the ground. If he passed out with his hand no longer sealing the wound, life would bleed out of him. Eric's mind raced. *Is this the end?*

He had been in tight spots many times. Always he had pulled through. The key was emotional control, never to be so frightened that he could not think and act. *Life's too good. I'm too young to die on this beach.*

He had to get around the headland where he could be seen. Clambering to his feet, arm still clenched, he staggered up the beach. "Suck it up, Eric," he told himself aloud. "Hike!"

Eric understood what was happening to his body. While in graduate school in Montana he had spent two years as a ski-patrol volunteer and had earned a certificate in advanced first aid. The skill had served him through nearly a dozen rescues.

After 50 yards, he slumped on his backside. He needed to put his legs up, get more blood to his vital organs, but there was no time. He rested thirty seconds and stumbled on.

Twice more he dropped to the sand in a half-faint. He felt the

blood pulsing under his hand, ready to spout. "Get tough!" he command-
ed, tightening his grip.

Ahead, 300 feet away, was a cluster of four beach houses. He stumbled toward them. Then he could go no further—he had to sit down.
Blood pooled in the sand around him. "Help me!" he cried.

In a small cottage at the edge of the beach, sixteen-year-old Ben Burdette
heard someone yelling. Stepping outside, he saw a man lying on the sand.
"Help!" came a shout. "I've been attacked by a shark. Call 911."

Ben saw the man's upraised arms were covered in blood. Turning on
his heels, he sprinted for the house.

Inside, Ben's mother, Michele, heard her son at the phone. ". . . on
the beach, bitten by a shark, looks pretty bad. . . ."

She ran to the beach. The figure sprawled there was still crying out.
She gasped at the gore of his legs and arms. Kneeling at his side, she saw
his lips were gray. "I'm losing it," he said. "You have to stop the bleeding.
My left arm. There's a pressure point underneath, up near the armpit.
Hold on tight."

Michele sank her fingers into the main brachial artery of the arm.

Seconds later, Ben was on the scene with towels. Following Eric's
instruction, he used them to elevate the wounded man's feet. Then he
raced off to flag down the rescue units. Michele avoided looking at Eric's
wounds and kept asking him questions to keep him awake.

In ten minutes or so, they were joined by a registered nurse, who
was also captain of the volunteer rescue squad in nearby Davenport, a rescue team from the California Department of Forestry and Nick Larsen.
He had been leaning against the truck, just a few hundred yards away,
suspecting nothing.

"It's good to have you here," said Eric as Nick gripped his hand.

The rescuers, soon reinforced by an ambulance crew, labored over
Eric for nearly an hour. They gave him pure oxygen and began running
fluids into his veins. Cutting away his wet suit, they bandaged his wounds
and pulled rubberized, inflatable trousers on his legs to force blood to his
upper body.

Rescuers were astonished he was still lucid after such massive blood loss. The first reading of his systolic blood pressure was a perilously low fifty. But by the time an evacuation helicopter got to the beach for the six-minute flight to Dominican Santa Cruz Hospital, Eric's blood pressure was close to normal.

It plummeted again with the removal of the pressure pants in the emergency room at Dominican, then began to rise after infusions of red blood and more fluids. Doctors judged that he had lost nearly half the blood in his body.

In the operating room, one surgeon worked on Eric's leg, another on his arms. The quadriceps leg muscle was severed, a piece of an arm muscle bitten out altogether. Both arms were laid open to the bone. The bone itself was scratched by the shark's serrated teeth. "It's like the bone was sawed with a bread knife," commented one doctor.

After five hours of surgery, Eric was wheeled to intensive care. Two hundred sutures closed his internal wounds, and 135 stainless-steel staples clamped the surface repairs shut.

A week later, he was home with a splint on his leg and casts on both arms. Three weeks after that he was limping along the beach and reliving his adventure. "I think the shark was tasting me, hoping I was a seal," he said. "Maybe he didn't like the taste of the rubbery wet suit and that's why he let me go."

Doctors credit his survival to unusual presence of mind and to physical conditioning. "People do amazing things when they have to," observes Dr. Andrew Nevitt, the emergency-room physician who first treated Eric at Dominican. "Eric is very athletic. Half strength for him is full strength for most men."

Eric is almost fully recovered and expects to be back enjoying rugged sports soon. "But there will be less time for them," he says. "My priorities have changed. Life is short. It can end at any time. I've always had confidence that I could accomplish something of real importance as an engineer. Now I think God is telling me to get on and do it."

SAVING JESSIE ARBOGAST

Timothy Roche

We've all heard the phrase "to take the bull by the horns." This story fea-
tures a triathlete who takes a full-grown shark by the tail and drags it
onshore, a remarkable effort that saved both the severed arm and the life
of a young boy. Such a bold, improbable rescue became sensational news in
Miami, more so when the hero refused all media interviews.

At dusk, two days after the Fourth of July, Jessie Arbogast was
having a Kodak moment on the beach in Pensacola,
Florida. The Gulf waves were mild, no higher than a foot
and a half. His sister and the other girls had ventured out
much farther, but Jessie, eight, his brothers, and some cousins stayed 15
feet from shore, crouched in the shallow surf. Then, one brother felt
something swish by his leg, and Jessie saw the sharp fins of a bull shark
protruding 2 feet above the water. The shark took an exploratory bite of
his arm and a chunk of his thigh. "He's got me!" Jessie yelled. "Get him
off! Get him off me!"

On shore, his uncle Vance Flosenzier turned toward the screaming
children and saw blood coloring the ocean. He and another man sprinted
to the surf and found the 7.4-foot, 200-pound shark about to roll away,
its jaw on Jessie's arm. Vance, who trains for triathlons, grabbed the shark
by its sandpapery tail and tried to pull, but it would not budge. He yanked
again, and Jessie fell away, his arm ripping as the shark clamped down.
Aware that two girls were still farther out in the water, Vance walked
backward, pulling the shark along the sandy bottom of the shallow sea
toward shore. With Jessie's arm only partly swallowed, the shark tried to
wiggle free from Vance's barehanded grasp. But Vance, at 6 feet 1 inch
and 200 pounds, held on and dragged it to shore where his wife Diana
and others had laid Jessie on the sand.

"Shark! My brother's been bitten by a shark!" a boy yelled as he ran down the beach. Tourists Trina Casagrande and Susanne Werton of St. Louis, Missouri, thought it was a prank and kept walking. Then they saw the chaos and the crowd gathered around the unmoving body of a boy, the red muscle of his thigh exposed and looking like a "bite [had been taken] out of a drumstick." The women could not see much blood. Most of it had drained from the boy into the Gulf. Jessie's lips were whiter than his face and body. His eyes were open, but rolled back.

"We have to get him covered up," Werton told her friend. All they could find were a sheet and beach towels. Werton took over CPR compressions from Vance as Diana blew air into Jessie's mouth. Werton counted to five, then pushed five times, then counted again as Diana blew. His chest rose, so they knew they were getting air into him.

The shark attack had severed Jessie's arm 4 inches below the shoulder. Vance tied towels into tourniquets and used T-shirts to cover the bone sticking out from the stump, slowing the loss of what little blood was left in the boy's body. Breathless but calm, Vance used his cell phone to call the 911 dispatcher, "The right arm and right leg are gone . . . completely gone. He's lost a lot of blood. . . . He wasn't breathing, and he didn't have a pulse a minute ago. . . . We need a life helicopter out here or something like that."

Before they landed, the crew of the chopper from Baptist Hospital saw the shark on the beach, its gray body against the white sand. Once the chopper touched down, they discovered that Jessie had basically been drained of blood, the worst situation in a trauma. In such situations, less than 1 percent of victims survive. No medication can help the heart. "There is nothing left to pump," says Greg Smith, an emergency-room physician who had hopped into the helicopter when he heard there had been a shark attack. "You've basically run the pump dry." The medics could well have declared Jessie dead. But Smith and paramedic Chris Warnock had kept the chopper's engines running for a "scoop and run" and with Jessie's uncle, they carried the boy to the chopper. "He was kind of like a rag doll," Smith says. Inside, the medics continued CPR and inserted a breathing tube. They had been on the ground less than six minutes. As they closed the door, they asked about the arm. Smith says, "No one knew where it was."

The shark was still thrashing on the beach. Jared Klein, a National Park Service ranger, wondered whether the arm was still in the water or in the shark's mouth. At a paramedic's suggestion, he took his expandable baton and pried apart the bull shark's jaws. There it was. But, says Klein, "the arm was too far in the mouth to remove it," particularly with the shark in such violent convulsion. He asked the crowd to step back and shot the shark four times in the head. Then he opened the mouth with his baton, while Tony Thomas, a lifeguard and volunteer firefighter, his own arm wrapped in a towel for protection, reached in with hemostats and extracted the limb. He covered it with a towel and packed it in ice to be rushed to a waiting ambulance.

By the time the chopper had landed at the hospital, Jessie had gone without blood—and thus oxygen—for thirty minutes. The medics put him on a gurney and took him down in an elevator four floors to Trauma Room 9, continuing CPR all the way. As doctors, nurses, aides and technicians hunched over the lifeless boy, nurse Dawn Colbert inserted an IV into his arm and began a rapid infusion of O-negative blood, the universal-donor type. Within fifteen minutes, Colbert pumped nearly 1.5 liters of warmed blood into Jessie, about half the normal volume for an eighty-pound boy. Jessie began to bleed. But his heart still wasn't beating on its own. Twice the team stopped CPR, waiting for Jessie's heart to pump on its own. No pulse. Nurse Sandi Miller, who was keeping watch for the arrival of the arm, prayed under her breath as the team continued CPR, then paused for a third time. One doctor felt a faint carotid pulse, another felt a femoral pulse. The blood began to flow on its own. Outside, the ambulance had pulled up. "As soon as his limb came through the door, we got a heartbeat," Miller says.

Having stabilized Jessie, Dr. Jack Tyson summoned colleagues to close up the wound. Joining Tyson in the ER were orthopedic surgeon Juliet De Campos and microvascular surgeon Ian Rogers. The doctors were surprised by the neat tears in the muscles and tissues. "My God," Rogers told the others. "This is replantable!" In sixteen years of reattaching arms, it was the cleanest cut Rogers had ever seen. "You never get a shark bite like that," says De Campos. Still, the doctors debated for nearly an hour before Rogers made the call to proceed.

One bone, three nerves, one artery, three veins, and three muscle groups had to be reattached if Jessie was to recover with some semblance of normal use of his arm. While De Campos prepared the stump, Rogers marked the corresponding veins, arteries, and nerves with sutures on the severed arm. First, De Campos shortened the arm even more, taking away about an inch of bone so that the stump would hold a plate to keep the limb in place. She clamped the bones together—two screws in the stump, two at the overlap and two more in the arm.

That done, Rogers connected the muscle tissue. Wearing magnifying goggles, he began reattaching major nerve endings, which are just slightly thicker than an eyelash. Next, veins and arteries were reconnected. Rogers had to take some veins from Jessie's leg to replace damaged vessels in the arm. Finally, Rogers released the clamps and blood began to flow back into the arm, which he describes as "absolutely white" and very cold. Arteries and veins starved for blood for so long went into spasms as new liquid began to flow. Antispasmodics were administered, and team members massaged the arm.

Five minutes, ten, fifteen. No response in the arm. "We were nursing this for about thirty minutes," Roger says. "Then all of a sudden, all the little cuts in his forearm started to bleed, and we could hear pulses in the arteries." The trickiest part, the doctors say, was stitching the skin back. "It was like putting a jigsaw puzzle together," says De Campos. After twelve hours in surgery, they wheeled him into the recovery room. They could only wait and see if he would survive.

Dave and Claire Arbogast found out about the attack when Vance called them from the rangers' station. It's the second time an Arbogast child has knocked on death's door. In 1994 Dustin spent more than a week in a coma after a car wreck. Now seventeen and recovered, he is the family's living hope for Jessie's recovery. Friends who know Jessie talk about a tough kid, one who can hold his own in debates with grownups about the sun and stars, but who is happy to shoot squirt guns and swing from oak trees. When he got a finger stuck in a hole in the school bus two years ago, he remained calm as firefighters cut away the bus to free him.

Last Thursday, thirteen days after the attack, Jessie's parents put him in a wheelchair and rolled him around the intensive-care unit, IVs dangling behind them. Jessie responds to pain stimuli, and his eyes are open. But his parents are not sure he can see them. At his bedside, they talk to him about Digimon cartoons and other things that he enjoys. The parents were there when De Campos moved Jessie's reattached arm to make him more comfortable, and the boy moved it back. They were there when he wiggled his hand. "They continue to view every small step as a very positive sign of hope," says Sister Jean Rhoads of Sacred Heart Children's Hospital, where the boy has been transferred. Rogers, Jessie's surgeon, says the boy will probably not regain full use of his arm. And his right thigh lost half of its mass during the attack, so he will probably require a brace to walk—if he can walk. Or if he ever wakes up to tell his part of a tale of a boy and a shark on the wrong side of each other.

Copyrights and Permissions

"Black December," by Tim Wallett. From *Shark Attack and Treatment of Victims in Southern African Waters*, published by Purnell & Sons Ltd., Cape Town, South Africa, 1978. © Tim Wallett, 1978.

From *Sharks and Survival*, edited by Perry Gilbert. © 1963 by Houghton Mifflin Company. Reprinted by permission of Houghton Mifflin Company.

Excerpt from *The Jaws of Death: Shark as Predator; Man as Prey*, by Xavier Maniguet. © First Lyons Press, 2001, Guilford, Conn. Originally published in 1991 by Editions Robert Laffont, S.A., Paris. English translation copyright 1992 HarperCollins Publishers.

"Bare Fists against a Shark," by Lt. Comdr. H. R. Kabat. Originally published November 11, 1944. Reprinted with permission of *The Saturday Evening Post*, © 1944 (Renewed), BFL&MS, Inc.

"Mona Island," by George A. Llano. From *Sharks: Attacks on Man*, originally published by Tempo Books / Grosset & Dunlap, New York, 1975. Reprinted by permission of George A. Llano.

"A Killer Gets Some Respect," by Michael Tennesen. Originally published in *National Wildlife* magazine, Aug./Sept. 2000. Reprinted by permission of Michael Tennesen.

"Shark Attack/Monterey," by Kief Hillsbery. Originally published in *Rolling Stone*, August 5, 1982. Reprinted by permission of *Rolling Stone*.

"In the Jaws of a Shark," by Peter Michelmore. Reprinted with permission from the December 1991 *Reader's Digest*. Copyright © 1991 by The Reader's Digest Assn., Inc.

"Saving Jessie Arbogast," by Timothy Roche. From *Time* magazine, July 30, 2001. © 2001 Time Inc. Reprinted by permission.